Praise for *This Is Motherhood*

"Motherhood is a vast up-and-down terrain where strength, joy, laughter, tears, doubt, and fear all come into play. In this beautiful collection of essays, mothers share the experience of becoming and being a mother, loving and letting go, struggles and triumphs. The book is a tribute to the incredible power of mothers and the all-encompassing nature of motherhood—it's a gift to mothers young and old, new or experienced."

DR. TOVAH KLEIN
a.k.a. "The Toddler Whisperer" + author of *How Toddlers Thrive*

"Each essay takes you on a beautiful emotional rollercoaster which ends at a destination that's nothing short of reassuring. It's raw, relatable, and oh so real—a must-read for mothers *and* fathers."

REEMA SAMPAT
actress, *Orange Is the New Black*

"This collection of essays and practices captures the richness of the experience of what it means to be a mother. Every mom needs a village—and this book reminds us that we're all part of the vital fabric of motherhood. The perfect gift for all mothers."

NATALIE GORDON
founder + CEO of Babylist

"*This Is Motherhood* is a delightfully encouraging read. This beautiful compilation of stories offers a glimpse into the hearts and minds of mothers who have traveled this path before us and alongside us to provide a faithful reminder that we are not alone."

REBECCA EANES
author of *The Gift of a Happy Mother* +
founder of Positive Parenting: Toddlers and Beyond

"Uplifting, empowering, and heartwarming: *This Is Motherhood* mothers the new mother, reminding her that there are millions of women who share her joys, sorrows, and triumphs. A perfect gift for the expecting or new mom."

NINA SPEARS
The Baby Chick

"So beautiful and thoughtful—a must-read for all new moms!"

CATHERINE MCCORD
author + founder of Weelicious

This Is Motherhood

This Is Motherhood

A Motherly Collection
of Reflections + Practices

JILL KOZIOL AND LIZ TENETY, FOUNDERS OF MOTHERLY
EDITED BY COLLEEN TEMPLE

sounds true
BOULDER, COLORADO

Sounds True
Boulder, CO 80306

Published 2019

Cover design by Rachael Murray
Book design by Beth Skelley

Photo credits: Crystal Sing-Giles, Raised Real, Anne Robert, Amy Soubannarath,
Juli Williams

"You Got This" © Motherly, Inc.

Printed in South Korea

Library of Congress Cataloging-in-Publication Data

Names: Koziol, Jill, author. | Tenety, Liz, author. | Temple, Colleen, author.
Title: This is motherhood : a motherly collection of reflections and
   practices / by Jill Koziol and Liz Tenety, with Colleen Temple.
Description: Boulder, CO : Sounds True, Inc., [2019]
Identifiers: LCCN 2018030473 (print) | LCCN 2018031508 (ebook) |
   ISBN 9781683643395 (ebook) | ISBN 9781683642657 (pbk.)
Subjects: LCSH: Motherhood. | Interpersonal relations.
Classification: LCC HQ759 (ebook) | LCC HQ759 .K688 2019 (print) |
   DDC 306.874/3—dc23
LC record available at https://lccn.loc.gov/2018030473

10 9 8 7 6 5 4 3 2 1

To the mothers who've come before us.
To the mothers who'll come after us.
And most especially—to the mothers who walk alongside us.
This is for you.

Contents

Mental Load

Love

Village

Strength

Magic

Welcome

Motherhood is a journey. Yet while becoming a mother is a path that is well worn, navigated by billions of women across the globe throughout human history, the experience is brand new for each woman every time a baby enters this world.

The first time you feel the thud of your baby's kick from inside your womb, the ache in your heart when your child is sick, or the mixed emotions of returning to work from maternity leave, motherhood is born in you anew. Each new frontier becomes an opportunity to learn more about yourself and your child, each struggle a chance to become a better version of yourself, each joy an opportunity to experience the rich sweetness that life has to offer.

Motherhood is an adventure that defies explanation; you just have to experience it for yourself.

It's real, raw, and powerful. It's beautiful and mind-blowing and monotonous. It's experiencing a total loss of freedom and gaining the greatest gifts on earth. It's finding our way on a path that's incredibly common and yet different for every woman. It's the most amazing transformation in a woman's life.

We're thrilled to be on this journey together. We founded Motherly because when we became mothers we saw a new wave of mamas redefining motherhood, owning what it means to be "Motherly" but unable to find the content or community that matched this optimistic, digitally native generation. It was as if the power of motherhood was an open secret, though many of the existing media outlets and brands seemed to be out of touch with this new generation of mothers.

We wanted to help write a new narrative about what it means to be Motherly, one that focused less on the conflicts of motherhood and more on celebrating the many creative paths that women are carving for themselves today.

You are Motherly . . .

You, the woman defining what thriving in motherhood looks like for you. You, the woman running an online business from home to have more flexibility for family life. You, the woman choosing to stay at home and give up alone time to gain years with your children. You, the mama continuing her education after an unplanned pregnancy. You, the working mom. You, the don't-label-me mom. You, the breastfeeder. You, the pumping mama. You, the formula feeder. You, the woman navigating the ups and downs of the tween years. You, the mama who worries that she won't love her second baby as much. (You will.) You, the lonely new mother in a new city trying to find her new identity.

Being Motherly today is not about focusing on what divides us or brings us down. It's about celebrating and empowering each woman's individual, triumphant journey.

Here's the secret: There are many ways to get motherhood *right*. There's no one way. It's not your mother's path or your sister's path or that seemingly perfect mom from your kid's preschool's path. It's yours alone. You get to define—and redefine along the way—your experience of motherhood. Your journey may not look the way you originally envisioned it, but it will be even better than you expected.

We wrote *This Is Motherhood* to be your companion on this journey. The book is organized by themes we all experience in motherhood—the firsts, the strengths, the depths, the magic—sometimes in the same day.

(Sometimes the same hour.) Although you may sometimes feel alone in your struggles and successes, mama, know this: You are not alone. The many stories told from women all over the globe, which are shared within the pages of this book, prove it.

The world is full of voices (sometimes our own!) telling us that we're not enough. That we're not doing it right. That we should try harder. That we must do more. These lies can steal the beauty from some of the most meaningful moments in our lives. We've had enough of those voices because they simply *aren't true*.

You are an incredible mother. Your choices are the right ones for your family. And you are enough.

We're here to inspire and guide you through some of the most miraculous and stressful milestones of your life.

This Is Motherhood includes reflections on this #momlife from mothers at all different stages of the journey: the soaring highs of meeting their new baby, the ground-shaking lows that made them doubt everything they'd ever known, and all the beauty and pain in between. To make sense of it all, we close each section with practices from our team of wellness experts to help you define, clarify, process, and celebrate your journey.

Motherhood is an opportunity to nurture—not lose—our true self. We hope this book feels like a loving friend whispering in your ear: "You're doing great. It's going to be okay. You've got this." Because you are. And it is.

You've *so* got this.

XO,

Jill + Liz

P.S. Welcome to #TeamMotherly. We're so glad you're here with us. Join us online at Mother.ly.

New Mama

Life is either a daring adventure or nothing.
HELEN KELLER

INTRODUCTION

LIZ TENETY

I was thirty-six weeks' pregnant with my first child when I realized I was just going to have to wing it. As my doctor was wrapping up my weekly appointment—measuring my swollen belly, checking my blood pressure, observing my vitals—I blurted out the burning question, which I was surprised she hadn't already answered: "But how will I know when I'm in labor? And what do I do when the baby's coming?"

My OB/GYN launched into her regular routine as she walked out the door. "Contractions get longer, closer together, and more intense. You'll call the office. We'll see you at the hospital," she said with barely a breath. Her words were ones she clearly had repeated a thousand times before. But didn't she know? Nothing about having a baby was routine to me.

I had been dutifully showing up for every prenatal appointment, expecting that my doctor would help guide me through this mind-blowing transformation that was occurring in my life. But as she closed the door with that "easy" answer about the signs of labor, the weight of motherhood hit me all at once:

My OB/GYN wasn't there to help me become a mom, to handle the psychological stress, manage the fear, or to even embrace the joy.

My doctor wasn't with me while I hunted for the perfectly safe car seat for my precious baby. She wasn't lying in bed with me, completely uncomfortable and entirely still—except for the life moving nonstop inside of me. She wasn't negotiating with me for maternity leave at work, wondering how I would manage. She certainly wasn't there to calm me when I woke up from my recurring pregnancy nightmare, where I forgot I had a baby and left my child somewhere. No, my doctor was doing her job—a medical job.

I realized in that moment that becoming a mother was a powerful transformation I needed to go through myself.

That's not to say I was alone. My husband was *so* supportive. My family was beyond thrilled. My friends were compassionate and curious. Although motherhood was a frontier that others had traveled, it was land I had not yet explored. I had read the pregnancy books but felt wholly unprepared. I was in my third trimester, but I wasn't yet "ready." And even though my son was on his way, I could barely wrap my mind around the idea that in a few short weeks, I would be his mother.

The journey to motherhood looks different for every woman. There are many ways to get there. It's vast and mysterious and beautiful beyond description. But it can be terrifying and even lonely.

In the years since my children were born, I have learned that none of us are really alone. The surreal feeling of the weight of motherhood does lighten, but it also returns, like when I watched my baby walk off to his first day of kindergarten or when I've gazed at my children sleeping soundly in their beds. How are they even real? It can just seem too hard to believe, a task too monumental to fully understand. And yet, we just show up, day by day. Lesson by lesson. Love by love.

So how did I know I was in labor? My first sign was when my water broke two days after my due date in the middle of our local CVS. Labor was nothing like I expected—and meeting my sweet son was immeasurably better than I ever dreamed.

Perhaps in your case, motherhood's reality sunk in on the car ride home from the hospital with your newborn baby. Maybe you found your stride the day your baby started sleeping through the night. Maybe you're still finding your way. And that's okay too.

Six years and two more babies later, I'm experiencing new frontiers every day. I'm still learning—and still winging it. But motherhood to me is the best adventure of all.

You've got this, mama.

P.S. This section is designed to support you through the massive change of motherhood. We've included an exercise at the end for you to write a letter to your baby documenting this special moment in time.

This Magic Moment

CAIT THRASHER

When I was pregnant with my first child, I took a birthing class with my husband. For hours we studied pain management techniques, watched videos of live births, learned where an internal fetal monitor was inserted, and contemplated other likely interventions, including medications. Our teacher was very experienced, and she answered every question we had, leaving nothing to our imaginations.

My husband and I wrote a birth plan, toured the hospital, packed our baby bag—and mentally prepared ourselves to throw our plans out the window. In the weeks leading up to labor I nested, I walked, I swam, I ate, I napped. I approached my impending labor and delivery in the way all the books and movies and busybodies at the grocery store tell you to: Plan, organize, and "sleep now because you'll never get to again!"

I was focused—and very, very nervous. But while my mind was busy turning over the possibilities of Pitocin and episiotomies, I forgot to get excited. Well, I was *kind of* excited, but as my due date came and went, I got crankier and more frustrated. Looking back, I wish I had let the feeling of excitement soak in more.

What most people forget to tell you as they regale you with how many hours they spent in labor, how many stitches they got, and how much pain they were in giving birth—is that the single most spectacularly wonderful moment of your entire life is going to happen on that same day!

In the seconds it takes for that last push to do its job and for you to set eyes on your baby, you will feel more happiness, triumph, wonder, and overwhelming awe than you've ever felt in your entire life.

Nothing is more physically satisfying or rewarding than giving birth to a baby. Nothing. It's hands down, without question, the best feeling in the world. And then—on top of your own personal physical miracle that you just performed—there is suddenly a brand-new, tiny human in the room. This little person is in command of your heart, and every worthy feeling you are capable of having. And you're new too! Now you're a mother.

I've spoken to my husband about it, who was there holding my leg (smartly not telling me what to do through my labor), and he'd tell you the same thing: Seeing our daughter for the first time was the most intensely awesome moment of his entire life.

This experience of becoming a parent has led me to believe that no matter how you meet your child—whether by C-section, surrogacy, vaginal birth, or adoption—the moment you do is one of the best of your entire life. And this feeling isn't limited to your first kid, which I learned after having a second child.

Even though I don't actually want more kids, I can't help but get a little jealous at the nine-months'-pregnant mamas I pass on the street. I love looking at them, knowing that the best day of their lives is just around the corner.

Labor is definitely difficult and painful and all the things everyone tells you it is, but I would gladly go through it *again and again* to get to experience *that* moment.

So, as you pack your hospital bag, or reread your pregnancy books, or find yourself worrying, take time to get excited! You're about to become a mother.

Birth Is Just the Beginning

JESSICA WIMER

Women often think that their worth as a new mom is defined by their birth experience and success with breastfeeding. A mom who planned for an unmedicated birth may be disappointed with herself when she's whisked to the ER for an emergency C-section. The mama who can't get her newborn to latch on may feel distraught and wonder if that means she's failing at motherhood.

Becoming a mother is not something that happens overnight. It's about much more than the first few moments and weeks with your baby.

Early on in your motherhood journey, it may feel like you've had to strip away all of the elements that make you who you are. As time trudges on, you realize that becoming a mother is not about losing your old self, but about blossoming into a new one. We emerge from the chrysalis of our former selves unsure if we're ready to embrace our new form and take flight. We struggle as we learn to fly. We hold on to who we used to be—and miss some of the possibilities that reside just over the horizon.

As we grind through sleepless nights and never-ending days wearing puke-stained yoga pants and a messy topknot to hide the fact we haven't showered in days, it feels nearly impossible to believe something vital has not been lost.

And perhaps life will never be the same. But mourning this loss would be as preposterous as a butterfly mourning the loss of her caterpillar self.

Great things are in store for you and that little baby. The promise of a future is nestled in your arms, and not just your baby's future. Yours too.

And the best part?

You get to define what kind of woman you're going to be.

I choose to define myself beyond my ability to mother my children, and this gives me peace during difficult parts of my day. I'm defined by my job and my role as wife, and by my love of nature, books, and cookies. I'm still an individual, and I need to connect with these other parts of myself to be able to share my light with the world.

While you're sitting in your mesh undies in a hospital bed or at home with a screaming toddler, remember: You're standing at the edge of a precipice. This is not an end. It's a place to launch yourself. Will you fly? I hope so.

With my young children, the days are *so* long and there are times it's nearly impossible to find any space for myself. Little hands clinging to my skirt hinder my flight. But that's okay. I like to smell the flowers. I will not be slowed forever. One day those little hands will be gone.

In this slower version of time, I am refining who I am, reveling in all sorts of discoveries that would have been left unearthed. Some are pretty. Some are not. At times I find myself grasping for composure as my once-never-ending supply of patience has run dry. Sometimes I am unkind to the two little beings who fill up my days with requests and reactions and cuddles and cries. But my kids have taught me the value of humbling myself when I am wrong. Their ability to forgive and forget is so foreign in my adult landscape. And my toddler has given me the ability to stop counting the minutes and instead soak in the moments.

While there are times I feel so restless that all I can think of is shedding my responsibilities and enjoying some well-earned freedom, I know, too, that motherhood is helping me become a beautiful new creation: the truest version of myself.

This Too Shall Pass

RASHA RUSHDY

The second time around, there were a lot of things I'd forgotten about having a newborn. Those first few weeks can truly be the most exhausting, the most challenging, the most painful, and the most terrifying. You wonder how your world has been turned on its head and whether it will ever be the same.

Repeat after me, mama: This, too, shall pass.

Last night, I spent two hours solely dedicated to settling my fussy twenty-day-old while her father got her two-year-old sister ready for bed. I envied his task—its predictability, its dependable routine, its lack of screams and cries, and the absence of self-doubt and desperation in those moments of *What do you want me to do?!* as I tried to figure out what this little person needed.

Those endless nights of wake-ups, marathon nursing sessions, never-ending diaper and outfit changes, spit-up, bedsheet overhauls, patting, shushing, and settling. Having to rock or bounce your baby with searing pain running down your back . . . all this will pass.

That excruciating, debilitating pain you felt shortly after delivery, just when you thought your recovery was going swimmingly, that made you think something was seriously wrong—made you question whether you were ever going to feel like yourself again . . . it, too, shall pass.

I'd forgotten what it was like to have to suddenly drop everything while caring for a newborn—dishes mid-rinse, laundry mid-sort, your shower mid-shampoo. Whether it's getting dressed, eating a meal, or getting some work done, you wonder if you'll ever have time to yourself again or be able to complete a task from start to finish.

But this, too, shall pass.

In the quiet of that 5:30 a.m. nursing session, everyone is still asleep except you and your new baby. Dawn filters through a crack in the curtains, dancing across those soft, perfect cheeks. In that moment, the world stops, and it's just you and your baby. You *somehow* fall in love with each other even more. You stare at her and wonder if she'll give you her first real smile today.

These moments, too, shall pass.

These moments, too, shall pass.

Even the nursing session, which you genuinely thought would never end until she melted her tiny body into your arms, peacefully exhaling her warm breaths on your neck, will pass. The days when all she wants is to lay on your chest, asleep and content to be close to the heartbeat that guided her for nine months, will be gone before you know it.

Your ability to be the person who can provide that baby with everything she needs—whether she's hungry, tired, scared, lonely . . . it will pass. There will come a point where you won't be her everything, the center of her universe.

I promise you, it will all pass, even the difficult parts of motherhood, the incomprehensible emotions, the sleep deprivation, the physical pain, and the lack of freedom and independence.

I can smugly say this because I've done it once before, mama. But I also know that those fleeting moments—those irreplaceable, perfect moments when you truly feel like this baby has made you a mother, to the point that you feel like your souls are perfectly in sync—will also pass. They don't disappear, but they change.

There's something special in the way a mother and her baby fall in love with each other, whether it's from that first moment you meet or later on. Just a few weeks ago, my toddler fell asleep as she laid her head on my chest. I realized she hadn't done that in so long, and I missed moments like those. There was a time when I desperately wished she wouldn't need to fall asleep on me, and you know what? It happened.

It passes. It changes. And I will miss it. I will deeply, desperately miss it.

From Surviving to Thriving with Twins

TANIKA WHITE DAVIS

When our twin boys were born, five weeks early and tiny as can be, I thought I was prepared. I had read all the books and quizzed all the mothers of multiples I could find. Yet actually holding them skin-to-skin on my chest changed everything. Suddenly all the fears and myths about twins overshadowed my preparation. I felt like a zombie walking out of the neonatal intensive care unit (NICU), stunned at the prospect of caring for two babies at once.

Should we sleep train? Would my milk come in enough to feed two newborns? Were these babies double blessings or "double trouble"?

I worried about losing sleep, losing myself, my marriage—maybe even my mind. I was overwhelmed with the thought of all the work ahead of me that would need to go into caring for both of my babies. And I really had no idea about the chaos that was about to consume our lives.

Eventually I learned that the only way my husband and I were going to survive twin parenting was by going through it. We're eight years in now, and we've learned a lot.

For one thing, I discovered that almost any superlative you use to describe your new state as a parent of multiples will turn out *not* to be the case. The fact is, you will sleep again. Will you sleep like you did when you were a college student? No. But you will get at least something that resembles a full night's sleep before your child is out of diapers.

People said our lives would eventually get back to normal. That wasn't true. Your lives will take on a new normal, but things will never be like they were pre-twins or pre-kids. Ever. The sooner you accept that you need to reimagine what "normal" now means to you, the happier and less resentful you will be.

As a sleepless and scatterbrained multiples mommy, I often thought I'd lose my mind. There may be times when you feel like you will too. The truth is, you won't. You won't always be doing everything at 100 percent capacity but that's okay, that's normal. You'll most certainly feel more forgetful, so you'll develop new organizational skills. And the stress of caring for two babies at once can eat away at the harmony in your house, so you'll work harder to keep the harmony by picking your battles and learning to laugh when you want to cry. Humor helps SO much. Graciousness with your partner helps even more.

At a certain point, I realized that just getting through the days— surviving twin parenting—wasn't enough. I wanted to thrive.

I didn't want to just "make it past" these tough moments. I didn't want to just "push through" these hectic years, like many advised. That was easier said than done, because having twins is, frankly, incredibly hard. There are fun moments, of course, but it is only double the fun for people who do not have to feed, change, soothe, clothe, and schlep two babies *at the same time*.

Being a parent of multiples can also bring double the anxiety, and double the stress, which means you and your partner have to be doubly good at communication. I look back now and see that my husband and I may have worked our best as a team when we had two infants. (AT THE SAME TIME!)

If I got a dollar every time someone said, "You sure have your hands full!" when I was out with a double stroller and a trunk-like baby bag, my income would look like Oprah's right now.

What we eventually learned was that our hands were full, but our hearts were fuller. Our lives were richer.

Our twin babies, who needed so much love, time, and attention, are now long-limbed, eight-year-old boys who need the same. There's a baby girl now, too, who is teaching us even more.

We sleep (most nights). We actually leave the house. We laugh a lot. We have a routine in place (most days), and sometimes our activities and adventures even go according to plan. I celebrate victories like a successful girls' weekend or a night's sleep without interruption because I know these moments are hard-won.

We survived then. And we're thriving now.

Perhaps you're not there yet. You may be knee deep in the chaos right now. You may cry at the end of the day because you ran out of patience and energy. You may feel guilty because you hurried bedtime or you wished for them to "just sleep through the night" or "just be able to walk" or "just be able to dress themselves."

I did those things too.

Eventually, over time, I learned a few things that helped changed my existence from surviving to thriving. I learned to cut myself a lot of slack. I learned to rest when I could, take time for myself, trust my instincts, and ignore the bullying twinges of guilt that taunt, "You're not doing as much as you can. You're not giving enough."

> You are giving it your best. You are doing as much as you can. Your babies are loved.

Even if you feel overwhelmed or like you're just getting by—know it's okay. The secret is, we *all* feel like that during the hard seasons. Those challenges, which sometimes feel absolutely overwhelming, turn us into amazingly capable, confident women.

Each ear infection, sleep regression, and bleary-eyed work meeting builds and instills a kind of mettle you didn't know you could possess. It's a process from surviving to thriving that happens step-by-step, day-by-day.

You are giving it your best. You are doing as much as you can. Your babies are loved.

You are enough. WE are enough. And we're doing an incredible job.

You Are Doing It, Mama

COLLEEN TEMPLE

I remember the first time my baby and I left our house together on our own. I felt like I was packing to go on an expedition around the world, like I didn't know when (or if) we'd return. I packed and repacked my diaper bag about ten times. I practiced opening and closing my stroller at least five. I dressed my daughter in the cutest outfit (well accessorized with a headband, of course).

I felt excited, but also a bit scared to leave. I just didn't know what to expect. I didn't know if the world had changed drastically since I'd last seen it. I didn't know if it would feel too big for us.

I also didn't want to look like I had no idea what I was doing. I wanted everyone to look at me and think, *Wow, look at that lady! That diaper bag has everything she could ever need! She is obviously a top-notch mom.* Or to not look at me at all because I was already so good at this that I didn't stand out like a sore thumb. I basically didn't want people to think, *This poor woman has no clue. Who allowed her to have a baby?*

Those first few weeks of motherhood are confusing. Even when I felt I was doing my best and getting through our day okay, there were minutes when I'd wonder, *Is this what I'm supposed to be doing? What are the rules? Where's the plan? The protocol? The procedure?*

Dear Sounds True friend,

Since 1985, Sounds True has been sharing spiritual wisdom and resources to help people live more genuine, loving, and fulfilling lives. We hope that our programs inspire and uplift you, enabling you to bring forth your unique voice and talents for the benefit of us all.

We would like to invite you to become part of our growing online community by giving you three downloadable programs— an introduction to the treasure of authors and artists available at Sounds True! To receive these gifts, just flip this card over for details, then visit us at **SoundsTrue.com/Free** and enter your email for instant access.

With love on the journey,

TAMI SIMON   Founder and Publisher, Sounds True

SOUNDS TRUE
many voices, one journey   800.333.9185

ST330

I quickly realized that my new gig was a learn-on-the-job situation, so I tried to do (for the first of many times) what felt right for me and my baby.

We used to stay in bed late into the morning after being up through the night together nursing. We'd say goodbye to my husband, who was off to work, and then drift back to sleep, waking again around 9:00 a.m. Sometimes I woke in a panic thinking I needed to be somewhere. It was all part of getting used to this "new normal."

We logged many hours on our couch—her breast-feeding, me binge-watching something on Netflix—an abundance of burp cloths and nursing pillows around us. These messy-hair-pajama-uniform days of postpartum life are bittersweet moments in time that I both yearn for and am proud of. Proud that we made it through that stage together. We were getting to know each other, we were finding our rhythm—in the comfort and privacy of our home. Our hibernation period was special; it felt sacred.

And then, just like that, one day I felt totally ready to emerge from our cocoon—in search of a connection to the outside world—so we went to lunch. As we entered the café, I felt nervous because it was just the two of us. I was scared I'd have to nurse her in public. I was afraid we looked out of place. I was obsessing over the fact that it seemed like everyone was staring at me, judging me. But you know what? Even though my stomach was in knots, we did it—together as a team.

So, to the new mama, out on an adventure with her little one: You are doing an amazing job.

So, to the new mama, out on an adventure with her little one: You are doing an amazing job.

You are out in the world with your baby. It can be nerve-racking, but that hasn't stopped you. And please don't let it! Because here's a little secret: We're all learning on the job. That's motherhood for you.

And you are doing it, mama.

Nowadays, as a mom of three who has taken my girls on many adventures, I wish I could tell my new-mom-self that the first step to any of this is believing in yourself. You *do* know what you're doing, because every day you're doing what's best for your baby.

Don't let the fear of not being perfectly prepared for every scenario stop you from getting out there.

No one is watching you to critique your mom abilities or waiting for you to fail. In fact, we're all still here, in the outside world, waiting to cheer you on when you're ready to step out of your newborn bubble. And you will, when it's time. But that bubble pops faster than any of us wants it to, so take as long as you need. Because the view is pretty beautiful in there.

The Chosen Ones

MARIA CONFER

My husband and I used to daydream about life with our future child—what it would mean for our lives, the things we'd do, the places we'd go, and most importantly that deep, unwavering love we'd have for our child. When the harsh reality of infertility changed our path to parenthood and we started our adoption journey, suddenly my heart was filled with fears that hadn't been there before.

Would I love my child the moment we met? How would I form that unwavering bond that I always dreamed of?

When you're already scared, an anxious, intense situation can compound your fear. This is what happened for me. When I mentioned my concerns to our social worker, she chipped away at my logic. She assured me that while "love at first sight" might not happen with our adopted child, it had no bearing on our future bond. Although her advice was sound and alleviated some of my fears, I still obsessed over whether we'd form a strong connection.

On the day our home study was completed, we received three expectant (birth) mother profiles. When I read through the second profile, I got goosebumps. I called my husband and told him this expectant mom was the one, that I *knew* it in my gut! It was love at first sight.

He was understandably hesitant and tried to calm me down, but when he called back ten minutes later, he agreed. She was the one we'd been hoping for.

Waiting to find out if we'd been chosen to be adoptive parents felt unbearable at times.

Did we dare hope and dream? Would she feel that same strong connection? As hard as I tried, it consumed my thoughts. As days turned to weeks, I didn't know how much longer I could endure the terrible feeling of uncertainty and anxiety.

Then one magical day—a day I'll remember for the rest of my life—the wait was over.

She chose us.

My heart still races and my goosebumps return just thinking about *that* moment. It felt as if my unrequited love for a family was finally reciprocated. It may be hard to understand, but we loved her from the beginning, and it was a true, real, and pure love. Over the past four and a half years, my love for her has continued to deepen and grow.

In the two short weeks we had to prepare for our son's birth, I continued to worry about how I'd feel when we met. Would the love magically happen like it did when we read his mom's profile? He didn't seem real yet, waiting in her womb, but *she* was real, and I already loved her so much.

His birth was a daze of high emotions. My son's birth mom and I held hands and cried together during his birth.

When the nurses handed me my son, I couldn't believe he was here. It was quite a surreal, strange moment.

Waiting to find
out if we'd been
chosen to be
adoptive parents
felt unbearable
at times.

I carried him to the nursery to get cleaned up and couldn't stop staring and crying. He looked so fragile and beautiful. I was in awe. I was in awe to be his mother. I was in awe of his birth mother's strength. I was in awe of his ten perfect fingers and ten perfect toes. I was in awe that he was mine.

In that moment, it no longer mattered whether or not it was "love at first sight." The awe overtook me and inspired my actions.

And as we built our trust, moment by moment, day by day, I discovered an awesome love. It's indescribable. But it's certainly a feeling *every* mother knows.

Love Carries On

LIZ TENETY

My maternal grandmother died a month before my first child was born. A week later, our family's former nanny, a surrogate grandmother who helped raise me, passed away. I attended their funerals that summer, my belly swollen with new life. Fellow mourners looked at me with eyes wet with sadness—and then smiled as they gazed at my belly.

Two months earlier both of these women attended my baby shower. They sat next to one another, catching up on family news, talking old lady stuff, and asking each other, "Can you believe Lizzy is having a baby?" None of us knew that in two months they would have both passed—one from a massive stroke, the other from a fast-raging cancer.

Yes, they were both in their eighties. Yes, they lived beautiful, full lives. But no matter how a person's story ends, it's always shocking. It's always so deeply sad. It's always so . . . final.

I was able to say goodbye to both of them as they lay dying in their respective hospital beds. Balanced there on the edge—between the imminent new life in my belly and the imminent deaths of these two powerful female forces—I took it all in.

I breathed in their legacies. I breathed in my dreams for my baby. I breathed in my emerging role as a mother, and the powerful breath filled the air, connecting the generations. I wished they didn't have to go. But I was profoundly grateful that a part of them would live on in my children—and that they were able to celebrate the next generation even in their final days.

One meaningful experience made it all so clear. At my grandmother's hospital, a sweet baby lullaby played over the loudspeaker every time a mother in the labor and delivery ward gave birth. Several times a day, as our family gathered to say our goodbyes, the sound of new life chimed.

At the end, there was a whole world of new beginnings. At the beginning, a reminder of the end.

I wasn't able to let myself wallow in my grief at that time because I was about to experience my own, profound life passage. And I knew, watching my grandmothers' descendants gather to mourn these amazing women, that a child—miraculous, unique, unyielding, and wild—was the greatest gift we could leave behind. I knew that this child would carry my legacy—and my mother's and my grandmothers'—into the future.

In the midst of setting up the nursery and registering for the right stroller and taking a birth class and timing my contractions came the most poignant of all reminders. *This* was it. *This* was what life was all about.

It's not about what you can take with you when you go or just what you leave behind. Life is about the real, vibrant love that creates and nurtures and pours itself onward into the future. It's a love that we and our mothers and our grandmothers quite literally carried within our bodies. It's a powerful love—cellular and cosmic—that forever carries on.

"Before we were conceived, we existed in part as an egg in our mother's ovary. All the eggs a woman will ever carry form in her ovaries while she is a four-month-old fetus in the womb of her mother. This means our cellular life as an egg begins in the womb of our grandmother. Each of us spent five months in our grandmother's womb and she in turn formed within the womb of her grandmother. We vibrate to the rhythms of our mother's blood before she herself is born. And this pulse is the thread of blood that runs all the way back through the grandmothers to the first mother."
LAYNE REDMOND

You Were Made for This

JUDIE HARVEY

Dear daughter,

You are a miracle, and nothing prepared me for how much I would love you. When you were born, the world stopped spinning for a moment. I was absolutely certain that God was in the delivery room. I felt connected to something much bigger than me, to the generations of mothers and daughters that came before and would follow.

Being a mom is both incredibly joyful and profoundly scary—sometimes simultaneously. You will experience the highest highs and the lowest lows.

Please know you are enough. You are strong, perfect, and right where you are supposed to be, even when it doesn't feel like it.

I know I'm your mom, and I'm supposed to think you're beautiful and perfect, but honey, you actually are. And just like I was chosen by some divine plan to be your mother, you will be the perfect parent for *your* child.

At times motherhood is overwhelming. Yet every time you feel overwhelmed, you're about to learn something. Spoiler alert number 1: You can't possibly know everything in advance. Sometimes you'll learn how to do something for the first time, like bathe your baby. Other times the lesson indicates that something in your life needs to change, whether that's your mindset, your environment, or something deeper.

When you feel overwhelmed because you don't recognize yourself anymore, you're about to learn that you haven't lost yourself, you're just *more* than you were.

When you feel overwhelmed because you're sleep-deprived and barely functioning, you're about to learn how to get your baby to sleep through the night.

When you feel overwhelmed because you can't balance work and being away from your baby, you're about to learn what's most important to you and how you want to structure your life.

When times are particularly tough, it's often a sign to simplify your life and not be so hard on yourself. Motherhood is hard enough, so don't make it harder! 'Cause, honey, motherhood is a *long game*. If you try to sprint your way through it, you'll wear yourself out. The hard, physical work of lugging, carrying, lifting, bathing, and endless holding (and nursing) ends eventually. She'll bathe herself and use the bathroom independently—and you'll use the bathroom alone for at least forty-five seconds (in a few years). Pace yourself.

I know you're a perfectionist, but you're going to make mistakes. Spoiler alert number 2: Motherhood will cure you of your perfectionism. Resistance is futile. I promise you, though, that when you look back, you'll see that you (mostly) made the right decisions. When you mess up, try to remember that you're part of something much bigger too.

> You won't always be able to see the big picture, and it's not always your job to find a solution.

You won't always be able to see the big picture, and it's not always your job to find a solution.

You'll feel more comfortable at different stages. It's not a sign of failure if you can't get the baby to burp. You may be the perfect person to teach her to read. Each phase comes with its challenges, and it seems like just when you figure out the current one, everything changes. In the beginning, your baby will change in increments of three months. Later it will be every six months, then twelve months, then eighteen.

I hope you enjoy every stage (like I did) and are grateful for the tantrums and outbursts. As long as your child is communicating with you, it's a good thing. And I found six-year-olds much more difficult than sixteen-year-olds, so don't fear the teen years!

As your child becomes a preadolescent, she'll be even more fascinating. Not in the sleeping infant way, but it's just as magical when she shows you her interests, passions, and a glimpse of who she'll become. Help her bring out these strengths to build her confidence.

Your body is precious—it can bring forth and nurture life—and I know you'll be tempted to run on empty to take care of your little one. Please don't. Take extra-special care of yourself in the fourth trimester—and for the rest of your life, too, for that matter. You were made for this!

Love,
Mom

practice
WRITE A LETTER TO YOUR BABY

DIANA SPALDING

Congratulations, mama! Welcome to motherhood. This is a big transition, and we want to help you acknowledge and honor all the feelings you have right now.

Maybe you didn't know how to deal with a blowout diaper at first, but now? I bet you're a pro. You're figuring this out—with that beautiful baby of yours—more and more every single day.

You may burst into tears because you're exhausted, and we want you to know that we did too. In any given day, you find yourself swinging from total self-doubt to complete self-amazement—and then back again. There are a lot of ups and downs on this ride, and it's more than okay to talk about the good and the bad.

In this chapter we invite you to write a letter to your new baby. This exercise is designed for you to take a moment to pause and reflect on this special, and oftentimes overwhelming, moment in time. We'd like this practice to help you honor the rich, colorful feelings you're experiencing each day by taking time to sit with your thoughts and write them down in an effort to support you in understanding the many ways you and your baby are affected in your transition to "mother."

Think about your child reading this letter in fifteen years—how amazing would that be? What do you want to document about this part of your journey? What do you want your son or daughter to know about the beginning of their life?

Here are some suggestions to help guide your letter writing:

- Outline what a typical day-in-the-life looks like right now.

- Describe what your little one loves to do and what makes them fuming mad.

- Convey your fears and hopes.

- Let them know about the first moment you *really felt* like a mom.

- Share what has surprised you most.

- Say what you feel most confident about.

- Name one value you hope to pass along to your baby, above all else.

- Share a hilarious story that will make you laugh for years to come.

Before you start your letter, find a quiet, relaxing space where you can feel free to write comfortably. Choose a time when the baby is sleeping or happily hanging out nearby. Allow yourself some focused time with your thoughts and enjoy communicating with your child through the written word.

And remember, mama: You've got this.

journal QUESTIONS

This is the first of ten journal sections that invite you to reflect.
If you enjoy journaling, here are some prompts to get you started:

- In what ways has your life changed since having your baby?

- When do you feel the most love?

- When do you feel the loneliest?

- What have you learned about being a mom so far?

- Who is your support system? How are you asking for help?

Firsts

Making the decision to have a child—it is momentous. It is to decide
forever to have your heart go walking around outside your body.
ELIZABETH STONE

INTRODUCTION

JILL KOZIOL

When I first became a mother, I was working as a strategy consultant. I approached motherhood like any other consulting project I'd previously managed, treating my impending new role like a research project. I used all of my normal coping mechanisms, including reading parenting books, taking classes, and asking for advice from those who had been there, done that.

But then I actually became a mom. And I quickly realized I wasn't in Kansas anymore. This wasn't like anything I'd ever done before (in the slightest), and my normal coping skills weren't enough.

There was *so much* contradictory information out there that my head was spinning.

I'd always looked for the *right* answer, the way you're *supposed to* do something, and I was surprised—a bit traumatized, even—to realize that there were many choices and no clear right way.

Was I a free-range parent? A Ferber parent? A "tiger mom?" Was I *Bringing Up Bébé*? I had no idea. As I started navigating this uncharted territory, I realized that I needed to figure out who I was before I could figure out what kind of mother I would be.

It wasn't until my daughter, Clare, was born and I heard her car seat snap into place for the first time that it clicked for me. I completely lost it in that moment and found myself sobbing in my husband's arms. It wasn't the fear of realizing the awesome responsibility of motherhood that caught me off guard. It was the realization that this wasn't a dream. I would get to keep this perfect little baby. She was mine, and we were in this together.

The good news is that all of my worry was for naught. Clare, my firstborn, and I figured it out together and are *still* figuring it out together more than seven years later. Our relationship, her needs, and the "kind of mother" I need to be are continuously evolving, and *that*, mamas, is a beautiful thing.

I remind myself that every stage she goes through for the first time, I'm going through it with her for the first time as a mother. From learning to breastfeed to teaching lessons on friendship after my daughter gets her feelings hurt by a classmate, I'm experiencing everything for the first time too. I'm figuring out how to guide her through these experiences.

As our children age up with these new situations, we grow alongside them as mothers.

Overcoming each new hurdle provides us both with a newfound confidence in the inner strength we both have.

As I've often repeated with both of my daughters, "I am strong. I am brave. I can do anything!"

And guess what, mama? So are you. And so can you.

P.S. This section celebrates the big and small firsts of motherhood: from the first time you realized your little one won't always need you the way they do right now to the first time you saw your partner hold your baby—and everything in between. At the end of the section, we invite you to try our mindfulness practice. It will encourage you to seek out the firsts that happen on a daily basis—the ones that fill your heart with love and your soul with happiness.

First Glimpse Into a World Without Me

ANNE-MARIE GAMBELIN

You left for school with barely a peck. I reached up to land one on your cheek as you scooted through the kitchen door. You don't want so many kisses anymore.

With teary eyes, wishing you needed me more, I watched you pull away. Although we'll always have our bond, it seems we've started to live life more on your terms.

I've felt this strange mixture of pride and melancholy before. Every time you declared, "Look, Mom! I did it!" you showed your independence. And each time was like a rubber band on my wrist, pulling *so* tight as I try to hold onto you, then snapping back—hot and sharp—when you let go. I feel the pain, and you feel the freedom.

But it's hard to imagine a world where you don't need me.

Your firsts have been lasts for me.

The first time you dressed yourself, choosing tie-dyed clothes to represent your individuality . . . *was the last time I could decide for you what suited you, literally and figuratively.*

The first time you put yourself to sleep at night was a sweet relief from the long nights of rocking . . . *yet it was the last time I was certain that all you would ever need to feel comforted and secure was me.*

The first time you rode your bike without training wheels . . . *was the last time you would need me for support and balance.*

The first time you had *your* friend over— not one I had chosen for you—and you two played in your own little world . . . *was the last time I could handpick your inner circle.*

The first time your friend's opinion had greater weight than mine . . . *was the last time you would accept my judgment without discerning for yourself.*

The first time you fibbed to me (it felt as though a spell had been broken) . . . *was the last time I could take every single thing you said at face value.*

The first time you wrote your name—the letters representing you, not me—your beaming pride saying you knew you were someone . . . *was the last time you would look to me to define you.*

The first time you put yourself to sleep at night was a sweet relief from the long nights of rocking . . . *yet it was the last time I was certain that all you would ever need to feel comforted and secure was me.*

It has all changed so quickly.

Now, when you are sleeping over at a friend's, I can't help flashing forward to you leaving for college. The quiet bedroom, rumpled bed, toothbrush near the sink, all reminding me that you are *here*, but that I have you on borrowed time.

Now you seek solutions through your own efforts, proving you can manage without me. You see your future draw near, instinctively preparing for the inevitable day when you'll head off into it.

While your independence takes the wind out of me, it places it under your wings.

And that's the way it's *supposed* to be. Even though these "lasts" hurt, each of these small and great milestones remind me that we're both on track. While I might not be ready for you to go, I *am* ready to watch you fly.

My First Day Back

LIZ TENETY

I wasn't supposed to go back to work. I didn't want to "leave my baby behind." I had heard that women "can't have it all," so I assumed that trying to manage "it all" was beyond my reach. Besides, I was barely used to the feeling of my firstborn child living outside my belly. Being away from him felt like a piece of my body was missing. It just felt wrong.

But at the time, I didn't have a choice.

My husband had resigned from his military service, and we didn't know if he was going to get a job or go to grad school. Since I had a stable job as a reporter, with health insurance and a steady paycheck, I had to go back to the office—at least for the time being.

With a sinking feeling, I packed up my things and headed to work for my first day post–maternity leave, leaving the baby with a hodgepodge of childcare providers and family members. I texted them constantly for status updates, counting the hours until I could get back to him.

I pumped barely enough milk in the lactation room and wondered if my baby's belly was full while I was away and if he was *finally* taking the bottle that he had so far refused. All day I felt a profound sense of unease—a pit in my stomach that wouldn't go away.

That first day, I was a most reluctant new working mother.

But as the days turned into weeks, and weeks bundled into months, something else happened. *I was doing it*. And my baby was thriving with his grandmother and auntie. My husband was even getting special bonding time with our son.

I wrote a front-page breaking news story, typing up the details while my son napped. I started finishing work tasks in mere hours that before the baby used to take me days. I interviewed a White House official over my cell phone during a major breaking news event while my son bounced in his swing beside me. (And neither of them ever knew.)

Since I was managing work better than I expected—something that actually shocked me because I didn't expect to "have it all"—my boss let me work remotely full time, and I have continued working from home for the past seven years, adding two more kids to the mix. This was *not* the story I expected to be writing about my professional life as a mother, but now I can't imagine it any other way.

Maybe your story is different than the one you imagined too.

Our society puts so much pressure on women to make the "right" choices around work, when in reality there are a million different ways for our families to thrive. Mothers are capable and accomplished, loving and nurturing, tireless even when they're exhausted. They deserve *so* much more than a world that makes them feel they can't have it all—or that they must do things a certain way to be the "right" kind of woman, to be the "right" kind of mother.

Let's give ourselves some grace and stop assuming we know what's best for others—and maybe even for ourselves. That amazingly brilliant woman who left an enviable career to care for her twins? She has never been happier.

That friend who leaves for work before the sun rises? She needs to work right now to pay off student loans but dreams of the day she can head back home full time. That nurturing mother who drops her kids off to day care? She finds her purpose in teaching her first graders how to read. That woman who isn't exactly sure of her career path? She's loving this more open phase of her life after decades spent chasing someone else's idea of success.

For the mama wondering how she will leave her baby to go back to work, I know your fears and worries.

But you can "have it all" because you get to define what that means. Embrace what you need for this season. Know that your story can change. And don't let fear, shame, or other people's expectations stop you from making the right choices for your family.

Our First Trip to the ER

JACQUELINE MUNRO TAPP

The morning after my son's first Christmas, I was still in my pajamas, living that holiday life, when I heard a dreadful sound. Without explanation, my ten-month-old baby, who had been playing nearby, appeared to be choking. As I called 911, I swiped in his mouth but found nothing. The EMTs arrived within moments, confirmed his vitals were normal, and said that any further step would be my choice.

In true first-time-mom fashion, I apologized for what was likely an overreaction. But I was unable to ignore a gut feeling. So my husband and I sped our son to the emergency room.

I just wanted to be sure.

As the X-ray images sprung up on the screen, the ER doctor delivered news that knocked the wind straight out of me: "Your son swallowed a safety pin. And it's open."

If I think back over my thirty years of life, this moment is the scariest I can recall. My heart was pounding as I looked at the X-ray in disbelief.

The surgeon would attempt an upper endoscopy. In short, my son would be put under, put on a respirator, and robotic tools would be lowered through his throat in an attempt to close and retrieve the pin.

The clock moved in slow motion as my husband and I held each other.

I focused on sending love and safety to my boy. After an hour and a half, I saw the surgeon and the anesthesiologist give us an excited thumbs-up.

I screamed and bawled, then hugged and chased after my son. Revisiting the relief, gratitude, and joy my husband and I felt in that moment will forever bring me to tears.

The pin, just a few centimeters in length, was red. It matched a tag from a pair of sweatpants, a gift given on Christmas. While I was cleaning up, the pin had landed somewhere out of sight. My son had found it and swallowed it.

Lucky for us, he happened to have some natural tiny-sword-swallowing skills.

I am forever grateful to the surgeon and medical team that worked on my son. And I'm grateful I listened to my gut that day. This was a true forged-in-fire moment for me as a mama, and I often joke that it has defined the relationship my son and I share. He is three now, and in the years since he swallowed The Pin, he's managed to scare me many more times.

My mama instincts tell me that these worrisome events my son puts me through won't be slowing down anytime soon . . .

Motherhood has brought me such glorious joy and affirmation, and it's also forced me to face fears too real to put into words. Becoming a mother has made me more vulnerable than I ever thought possible, for I now know how it feels to see my heart travel outside of my body. We are given this precious gift of our children, and with that gift comes the challenge of balancing an all-consuming love against the creeping fear of worry.

It is difficult to see our children suffer—that becomes abundantly clear with the first tears, the first shots, and the first falls. I'm still learning that we can't control everything that happens to our little ones. I know my son will face pain and hardships as he navigates his life. I know that the best I can do is to try to guide him; to love him with my whole, open heart; and to trust in my motherly intuition along the way.

Because what I'm finding is, if I tune in, the "eternal knowing" is inside me, and the messages are clear and loud and, most importantly, they are true.

The First Time My Baby Hurt My Feelings

LIZ TENETY

My baby was fifteen months old when she tried to hurt me.

I was busy one morning wrestling her into her car seat, pulling the straps around her shoulders. As I looked down, her round face was flushed red and trembling with rage—she was absolutely infuriated that I was doing this to her. For the very first time, she was showing me just how upset she could be. She reached her chubby hand out, grabbed my finger, and bit me.

In an instant, we entered a new stage.

It was a shock to see my baby so upset that she was trying to hurt me. How could this sweet, small human who I doted on 24/7 actually be mad at me? My shock quickly melted into amusement—even gratitude.

My baby was growing up, and that's a good thing.

It's natural—even good—for her to express her own feelings and thoughts, within limits of gentleness and kindness.

It's natural—even good—for her to recognize the autonomy of her own body and to let others know when she's not being respected.

It's natural—even good—for her to assert herself with her parents. It's just hard to be the one she's pushing against.

Of course children naturally test limits—and it's the parents' responsibility to know when to hold firm and when to yield to the next stage.

But those firsts can be quite bittersweet.

- The first time your child calls you "Mom" instead of "Mommy."

- The first time your child marches into a play date and doesn't look back.

- The first time your child wants to dress themselves.

- The first time your child refuses to kiss you at the school drop-off.

- The first time your child has a difficult problem that they want to solve on their own, without your help.

Growing hurts, but that pain can be good.

Growing hurts, but that pain can be good.

When I look to the future, I want my children to thrive as unique, independent, free, and competent adults. But between now and then, there will be a million tiny cuts to the tethers that hold us. And I know that each cut will sting.

These little detachments won't look like I expect. They will be my toddler biting me when she doesn't want to be put into her car seat or my son picking the *most* ridiculous outfit to wear to school—backward—or me staying up late worrying about why my teenager isn't answering my text messages.

With every new freedom, there will be a little pain too. We won't always get it right. They'll cross the line, my babies. I'll overreact—or overprotect. They'll terrify me. I'll annoy them. It's just so hard to figure out when and how to let them go because, in the end, the ties between us won't be as visible. My son won't need to hold my hand when he crosses the street.

He'll soon pack his own lunch and fill it with whatever he likes. In college, he won't worry if I miss him when he decides to spend Christmas break with his girlfriend's family instead of his own.

But the gift of children who *know* they are safe and cherished, those are the ties that remain. And someday, maybe when they become parents, perhaps my kids will finally understand. This kind of love hurts and heals and creates and grows. It's a bond that will ache with love, now and for the rest of my life.

Our First Day Alone Together

KARELL ROXAS

It's Monday morning, and my husband is about to return to work after two weeks with us in our newborn bubble. I have no idea how today will go. I repeat to myself, *By tomorrow I will have cared for the baby on my own, and it won't feel so terrifying*. But can I really manage?

Two short weeks ago our son was born, and the three of us had been in an endless cycle of swaddle, sleep, wake, feed, hold, change, cuddle, and repeat. Sleep feels like a hallucination—something I *swear* is real, but I can't really tell you for sure.

I suddenly realize I'll be entirely alone for a whole day with a little creature who needs me to protect and feed him to keep him alive. The weight of this responsibility suddenly feels heavy. *I am a grown-up and also a mother*.

Who let this happen?

As my husband leaves, I admit I also feel jealous. Our morning routine used to include my husband and I walking to the subway, each of us calmly sipping our coffees, then breezily exiting the train to our respective offices. I miss the real (work) world, with its predictable routine of work, lunch, and a 3:00 p.m. coffee break—where no lives are at stake and showering each morning is a given.

I loved my job and the work I did. I knew what I was doing, and I was good at it. I answered my team's questions and multitasked, set deadlines, and followed through. It was a choreographed dance I knew well. Then, in two short weeks, that familiar routine, personal identity, and sense of accomplishment I once took for granted had been completely upended by this new life where I'm brailling my way through every moment and figuring it out as I go. Hello, humility . . .

I stare at the clock. Only thirty minutes have passed since my husband left. *How will I ever make it through today?*

> I wonder whether I'm mourning my past self or coming to terms with what motherhood is really like.

I hear my son cry and am grateful to know what to do next. As I feed him, I think, *You know what to do. Burp him.* As I concentrate only on the next step, the day feels less overwhelming. We move on to a diaper change. I am already less awkward with these than I was two weeks ago. His kicking legs don't throw me off anymore, and I can change him quickly and easily.

I'm not sure what to do next, so I grab a book to read. Although I feel silly reading *Goodnight Moon* out loud to essentially myself, I look at my baby and he seems to be listening. Eventually, he starts to look sleepy, so I swaddle him, rocking him slightly until he falls asleep.

I barely did anything, and yet it feels like such an accomplishment.

The rest of our day is filled with these tiny victories. I sing to him as we make my lunch together. We do tummy time and bath time and many diaper changes. The fear starts to ease.

As I hold on to my sweet boy, I'm suddenly overcome with conflicting feelings of love and overwhelm. The love I feel hits me like a force, surprising me with its immensity and power. But there's something else present too—sadness. I wonder how it can creep in among all the love.

I wonder whether I'm mourning my past self or coming to terms with what motherhood is really like.

It has been three years since that first day together, and while each day has brought new challenges, it has also brought more victories.

These happened slowly, but I got better at being a mama without even realizing it. I still question my decisions from time to time, but my confidence has grown immensely. I know better than anyone else what my child needs to grow and thrive. And now no one can shake that fundamental belief.

I am a grown-up and also a mother. Yes, I am.

The First Time Seeing Him as "Dad"

COLLEEN TEMPLE

I'll never forget when my husband kissed me or said "I love you" for the first time. I'll never forget the thrill of hearing, "Will you marry me?" or looking into his eyes as we promised to love each other forever. And I'll never forget the look on his face when I told him I was pregnant for the first time.

Similarly, those first few moments after I delivered my daughter are seared into my memory. I'll never forget feeling my baby's small, warm body on my chest or when our eyes locked for the first time as we pulled her into this world. "I'm your mama," I said excitedly through the happiest of tears. It was miraculous and unbelievable and exhilarating all at once.

I wanted to remember every second of it.

I loved my husband for 189,216,000 seconds before our first little girl arrived. And I carried that beautiful child in my womb for 24,278,400 seconds. But it only took *one second*—when time froze and our baby entered this world—for us to become parents.

The first second that I knew I loved this man, I honestly didn't think I could love him more. I was fully on board the all-consuming roller coaster that is falling in love. But then we had a baby together. And it took just *one second*—one quick glimpse of seeing my husband proudly hold our daughter in his arms for the first time—for me to fall even deeper in love with him.

Whoa, look at them, I thought proudly. We just created a family.

It took just one second while I watched my husband learn how to wrap our daughter up in a swaddle—as she wrapped him around her finger—for me to realize that he was going to be the best father in the world.

After that, he continued to impress me with his dad skills. I mean, watching your husband dance to "When Will My Life Begin?" from *Tangled* for the millionth time with your daughters just does something to your heart.

Since our first baby, we've spent many seconds of our lives changing diapers, soothing crying spells, kissing boo-boos, and playing dress-up. Our family has grown to include two more daughters, and our hearts to include so much more love. We have spent endless seconds worrying if we're doing anything right, feeling overwhelmed with being in the trenches of parenting young children.

> The "firsts" in life are wonderful—and fleeting. They may happen in a split second, but they are treasures that we'll keep safely tucked away in our minds for eternity.

There's a lot to figure out, and a lot of growing up to do once you become parents. That takes years, *not* seconds—which we are figuring out together—little by little, every day.

The "firsts" in life are wonderful—and fleeting. They may happen in a split second, but they are treasures that we'll keep safely tucked away in our minds for eternity.

Time is a funny thing. We spend so much of our lives wishing for it to speed up, wishing for the next exciting thing to come along, wishing to fast-forward through the hard or boring moments of life. But when all is said and done, I'm going to look back on this time in our lives—of us figuring out how on earth we're supposed to do this gigantic job of raising good people—with a deep love, abundant joy, and, I'm sure, an aching heart.

We'll have new firsts, my husband and me. They'll be sweet, I'm sure. But I'm not sure any could compare to watching him with each of our daughters on the first day they met.

The First Day
of Kindergarten

LIZ TENETY

My love,

You're entering school, and it feels as though it's the end of our "young years" together. Today I'm remembering what these last few years have meant. Five years doesn't seem that long ago, but we've accomplished so much. And that makes my heart swell, so much so it may burst out of my chest. A wonderful world awaits you, but this new beginning also closes the chapter on the baby years.

Kindergarten is here, all too soon.

School starts now—and so do friendships, homework, and long days outside our home. Kindergarten is the launching point of your life beyond our family. And that's a very good thing, but it's a bittersweet thing too.

As you begin this journey, I have many hopes and dreams for you.

I hope you learn . . . about the beautiful people in our diverse world, and find your place within it . . . that you find friends who laugh at your jokes, let you into their secret clubs, and invite you to their birthday parties . . .

I hope you appreciate all the effort the adults in your life put into teaching, guiding, coaching, and supporting you . . . that when you find out about the difficult times that your family, friends, country, and world have been through, your heart is moved with empathy and stirred to action.

I hope that when you encounter a roadblock on your journey, you don't see it as a reflection of your worth, but an opportunity to try and discover something new, push yourself to your limits, and discover something about yourself. I hope you learn there's no substitute for hard work and discipline even when you want to take the easy way out. And that along your journey you unlock the creativity inside of you and express the many facets of your personality in a way that speaks your truth.

I hope you see your siblings looking up to you and that you reach down to show them you care. They admire you and adore you—don't forget them as you launch into your own little world. And while you're off conquering the world, I hope you find ways to slow down, unplug, and look within—to pray, to meditate, to contemplate—in silence (especially since you're growing up in a time of computer screens and digital addiction).

I hope you learn to do hard things, such as stand up for the kid others are picking on; go out of your way to do the inconvenient, right thing; or take on some task others are overlooking. I hope you enjoy the (mostly) innocent world of crushes, and that someone will sweetly crush on you. Those feelings of love and longing make the future seem magical and wonderfully full of possibility.

You're going to do amazing things. We're already *so* incredibly proud of you.

Know that I will do everything I can so that home is always your safe place. We've loved you before you were born.

Always,
Mama

practice
MINDFULNESS IN DAILY LIFE

RACHEL GORTON

Wouldn't it be wonderful if you could start each day alone, overlooking the ocean with a cup of coffee or meditating quietly in your garden? Or maybe journaling while cozied up in bed with a cup of tea sounds like perfection to you. Whatever your ideal scenario—if it were possible, it might help you have a deeper sense of calm to carry with you throughout the day.

As a mother, your mornings probably don't start out quite like that. Instead of calm there's chaos, instead of peace there's exhaustion, instead of timeliness there's rushing. And while it might not be feasible to take a few moments alone, you *can* bring mindfulness into your day and practice the art of being present.

Set a goal to be mindful today and throughout this week. Notice (without judgment) how your body feels upon waking. Are you tired or achy? Are you feeling great? Allow yourself a few deep breaths—in and out—before your feet hit the floor, and remind yourself that today is a new day.

No matter how overwhelmed you feel or how long your to-do list is, you can set aside this time to observe your life and your children and to simply notice.

Notice your child's first facial expression of the morning. Notice the warmth of your first sip of coffee or tea and how the steam feels on your face. Notice the feeling of your child's body and weight in your arms. Feel the warm water and soap on your skin as you wash your hands for the first time today. While the big firsts in your child's life play a significant role in making memories and reaching milestones, you'll discover many other firsts if you allow yourself to be in the moment.

As you shift into mom mode for the day, observe your child through the lens of curiosity. Does she want to be close to you or to play independently? Is he trying something new and waiting for your encouragement?

While you explore this concept of being present, what are you recognizing about your child? Do her facial expressions change when she is really focusing on something? Do his eyes narrow as he scans the pages when you read books together? Does his voice change when he gets really excited?

As mothers, we need these mindfulness skills to refocus our attention where it is needed most.

We all need those gentle reminders to live in the *now*. In difficult times, stop and ask yourself, "Am I here?" "Am I experiencing this moment?" Sure, some of these moments will include piles of dishes and unfinished tasks at work, but when you are fully experiencing your life, you see with a new level of depth and awareness.

We invite you this week to take the time to find stillness each morning and create a rhythm of coming back to the present and noticing what's before you . . . in all its guts and the glory.

Your attention may wander, and you may forget to call upon this practice, but that's exactly why it's called practice. At any point in the day, mindfulness can help bring you back to the present and provide a new opportunity to spend beautiful, undistracted moments with your children and your life.

It's these everyday moments that make up our entire lives—may we revel in them together, mama.

journal QUESTIONS

- As you reflect back on your experience of motherhood, which firsts are most memorable to you?

- As you work with finding stillness each morning and becoming mindful of the present, what tiny firsts have you noticed this week?

- How can you take more time to notice your child and yourself experiencing these things?

Mental Load

Let no one ever come to you without leaving better and happier.
Be the living expression of God's kindness; kindness in your face,
kindness in your eyes, kindness in your smile.
MOTHER TERESA

INTRODUCTION

LIZ TENETY

Mothers always leave the world around them a little bit better than when they found it.

Whether it's a boo-boo miraculously healed by mama's kiss, a kitchen sink full of dishes that only *she* seems to wash, a work project that *has* to get done (as they say, if you need something done just ask a busy mama), or a first birthday party that's not going to plan itself (Pinterest, for the win!), one of the most amazing things about mothers is their ability to transform the world around them for the better.

It's almost part of the commandments of motherhood: *Thou shall leave things better wherever you go.*

But all that doing can be absolutely, relentlessly exhausting.

There's the physical work of pregnancy and breastfeeding, of day-care drop-offs and preschool pickups, of cleaning and cooking—and then cooking and cleaning again—of bathing and cuddling, and putting the kids back into bed. For. The. Last. Time.

There's the mental load of remembering all the things you need to do, like schedule the two-year checkup, fill out the camp forms, add playdates to your calendar, pay the bills, get the car inspected, pack the lunches, bring the snacks to preschool, do the laundry (again and again)—not to mention the constant worry that something could happen to the kids.

Oh, the worry. Oh, the to-do lists.

There are the 2:00 a.m. nursing sessions, the 6:00 a.m. wake-ups, and the 8:00 a.m. drop-offs . . . the 11:00 a.m. work call, the 2:00 p.m. pleeeease-take-a-nap time, the 5:00 p.m. dinner rush, the 7:00 p.m. bedtime shuffle, the 8:00 p.m. cleanup, and the 9:00 p.m. work check-in.

And the—*we forgot to take the trash out!*—midnight action.

In all of the chaos, it's easy to forget that someone you know quite well also needs some love, attention, and respite: *you.*

Mama, you are a person too.

In the midst of the mental load of motherhood—the burdens that must be shouldered, the tasks that must be done, and the love that will be given so generously—it's easy to put ourselves, even our basic needs, last on the list.

While the load can be extremely heavy, we hope you find ways to shift some of the burden, to give yourself credit for the thousands of thoughtful tasks you do, to be open with your partner about how to best divide and conquer responsibilities, to advocate for your needs at work, and yes, to even prioritize time to care for yourself.

Because *you* make everything better, mama. So now we want to help make motherhood a little bit better for you too.

P.S. We've included a wellness checklist at the end of this section to make it easier for you to be accountable for taking care of you. Drink your water, find your Zen, and start your day with your favorite song. Mama? You've got this. (And we've got your back.)

The Beauty and Purpose of Monotony

COLLEEN TEMPLE

My cute five-month-old alarm clock went off this morning. I scooped her up and brought her into my bed to nurse. As she drifted back to sleep, I headed to the kitchen for coffee. My two older daughters woke up shortly after, asking where we were going today *and* if they could go outside *and* if they could watch a show *and* if they could paint.

And so . . . the day begins, much like it does every morning.

After the bombardment of questions and requests, I cook breakfast. We eat, and then I clean up the mess. I assess what needs to get done today, answer work emails, and complete certain time-sensitive tasks.

Then we pick out outfits—I help where I'm needed—and when I find time, I throw on today's version of my uniform—likely black yoga pants and a "fancy" sweatshirt. Sometimes there's a shower, sometimes there's makeup involved, sometimes I comb my hair—and I always brush my teeth. (Wait—I *did* brush my teeth today, didn't I?)

But, mama, there is beauty in this monotony.

Every day I change multiple diapers, nurse my baby (what feels like) a million times, help my kiddos brush their teeth, put shoes on and off, get them in and out of car seats, find pacifiers, calm tantrums, cook and clean up, drive kids to and fro', wipe boogies, comb (gently, as instructed, of course!) hair, help find things, sing songs, play I Spy, take direction, give direction, do the bedtime dance, and go to sleep.

Then I wake up and do it all again the next day. And the next. And the next. I do so much of the Same. Exact. Stuff. Every. Single. Day.

But, mama, there is beauty in this monotony in our lives.

There's beauty in those teaching moments . . . You show your daughter how to tie her shoes—again and again, day after day.

There's beauty in how you care for your children . . . You so lovingly feed your baby whenever she's hungry. Even if it's at 7:00 p.m., 10:00 p.m., 1:00 a.m., 4:00 a.m., and 7:00 a.m.

There's beauty in your gentleness when you coach your toddler through a meltdown (even if it's in the middle of Target or church or someplace you'd actually *really* rather it not be happening).

> But, mama, there is beauty in this monotony in our lives.

There's beauty in the millions of tiny magical moments that we get to experience over and over too.

I get to hug my kids and relish in these enthusiastic bear hugs that make my soul sing.

I get to receive fifty kisses a day from my children. Big, sloppy, happy kisses that make my heart skip a beat.

I get to show my toddler how to do things for herself. Every day I get to guide her in becoming a strong, intelligent human who can do so much.

I get to answer questions from my curious preschooler. I get to teach her about the world around us and how things work—like why flowers grow in our backyard and what it means to be a good neighbor.

I get to feed my strong, healthy baby girl from *my* strong, healthy body. I build her immune system, strengthen her muscles and bones, and put her needs before my own — teaching *me* how to be selfless and compassionate.

I get to read bedtime stories, say prayers, and tuck my babies in to sleep. And every night I get to check on them — watching their full bellies rise and fall — while they drift off to dream world.

I get to tell my children I love them.

Best of all, I get to play a part in shaping the lives of three very special little girls. It's not an easy task, but it's a worthy task. And I try to remind myself that this monumental, life-shaping work is done moment to moment, task by task, day by day.

In my own little world, I do a lot of the same things and I face a lot of the same challenges, but when I am able to see the big picture more clearly, I remember that this sameness is actually me actively shaping the lives of tiny humans. That's no small feat.

It's easy to get caught up in the chaos because this work of motherhood is just plain hard (and tedious). So let this be our reminder: Even when it feels monotonous, it's *actually* monumental.

No, You're Not Doing It Wrong

DIANA SPALDING

As I was leaving a mommy-and-me gym class, I was carrying the car seat with my newborn in one hand while holding my toddler's hand in the other. I opened the car door, and my toddler made a beeline for the parking lot.

By some marvel of mama power, I was able to grab him before he ran in front of a car—and without dropping my newborn—but not before falling, tearing my pants, and skinning both knees. I was relieved he was okay, but in that moment, I felt so tired, so defeated, that I sat down on the sidewalk and cried. A mom from the class I'd just left—someone I barely knew—knelt down next to me and put her hand on my back.

"You're not doing it wrong," she said. "It's just *that* hard."

In that moment—with my hair matted to my tear-soaked cheeks and searing pain shooting down my legs—she made me realize it wasn't my fault. I could try as hard as I possibly could *every* day, but sometimes life would just be messy.

We often believe that if something isn't going right, it's our fault. We wonder: *Am I missing something that would make this easier? Other moms seem*

And so,
darling mama,
allow me to
pay it forward.

to have this figured out, what's wrong with me? If only I was [fill in the blank]-er, I wouldn't be facing this problem.

You spend hours a day washing, folding, and wiping, but every evening your floors are still covered with Legos, crumbs, and tiny socks. You read books on sleep, try everything you can think of, and your baby *still* won't sleep through the night. You love your children so much it hurts, yet you check the clock repeatedly to see if it's bedtime. And every time you cross something off your to-do list, you add two more tasks that need your attention.

And all the conflicting parenting advice you get makes you question your own parenting decisions.

Am I doing it wrong, or is it just hard?

Mama, it's hard.

You desperately miss your partner, but find yourself collapsing into bed—alone—because you are just too tired out to consider anything romantic.

Perhaps you love your job but can't devote your attention to it the way you used to. Or you really dislike your job but can't leave because of the money or insurance or tenure. Maybe you love being a stay-at-home mom but are sick of feeling as though you have to defend your choice to everyone. Or you thought you wanted to be a stay-at-home mom but find it's not what you envisioned.

You're not doing it wrong, it's just *that* hard.

And so, darling mama, allow me to pay it forward.

In that moment, when I felt like a complete and total failure, a stranger saw an exhausted mother who was trying *so* hard to take care of her kids that it left her bleeding and crying on a sidewalk. She saw me clearer than I could see myself.

Finding time for yourself when you are a mother is just hard, and so is working on your relationship. Keeping the house clean, making parenting decisions, getting stuff done, figuring out how to balance . . . all of it is just plain hard.

Not because you are doing it wrong, simply because it *is*.

The fact that you keep going, keep cuddling, keep cleaning, keep planning, keep working, and keep loving *in spite of* how hard it is, is your superpower. You're doing the hardest job on the planet with dedication, grace, and love. And there is nothing *wrong* in that.

What Is Balance Anyway?

JESSICA JOHNSTON

I spent a long time learning to forgive myself for falling short of what I thought I needed to do and be. But the truth is, motherhood is going to look different for all of us. The concept of "balance" is going to look different for all of us too.

Balance means letting go of my concept of the perfect motherhood and accepting a messy, imperfect, *real* version of being a mom.

Sometimes motherhood feels like juggling hot potatoes. When I'm at work, I feel pressure to be with the kids. When I'm snuggling them, I feel suddenly compelled to vacuum the house too. It's just not possible to do it all.

I haven't seen the bottom of my laundry basket in years. *Literally* years. I clean my house, but I barely ever clean my microwave, fridge, or shower. If we are going to be friends, you need to know that.

Balance at my house looks something like sit-down dinners of mac 'n' cheese from a box. It looks like takeout on the long days. Or putting my feet up and eating chocolate after I sing the last bedtime song and retrieve the last glass of water.

The lie that we can somehow do it all will kill our joy *and* our spirits. Maybe the answer is found by trying to figure out what "it all" means to us.

I'm in awe of the naturally minded mother. I salute the mom who loves to sit down with her kids and teach them about life and outer space. I'm impressed with the mom who always looks like she and her kids walked straight off an Instagram feed. I'm a little jealous of the mom who never raises her voice, even when her kids are engaged in a Mach 7 tantrum.

I high-five the mom who takes care of herself. I appreciate the house that is always clean with something baking in the oven. I learn from the moms who are constantly researching and learning. I honor the single mom, the working mom, and the stay-at-home mom.

I have watched my friends sacrifice their bodies to grow, feed, and care for their children, and I think each and every one of these moms is beautiful in *her* expression of motherhood.

It is a most honorable calling, whatever way we choose to do it and however we manage to balance it all.

You see, I *know* how hard this job is. I *know* that we don't get to "be it all" or "do it all" or "have it all" without losing ourselves (and even then, something's gotta give). This job is exhausting physically, mentally, and emotionally. It takes all we have *and more*.

> Balance is doing our own brand of motherhood and letting the rest go.

Balance is doing our own brand of motherhood and letting the rest go.

For me, balance looks like answering a thousand questions in an hour and ordering nachos tonight for dinner.

Sometimes, when I'm getting work done while my kids entertain themselves (read: wrestling, arguing, and Netflix), mom guilt whispers in my ear: "You're failing them, you should be present right now. Put your work down."

The other day, instead of ignoring this nagging feeling, I looked up from my work and asked the kids if they felt neglected by me. "What?!" my oldest said in shock. "Mom, you're working, we are *fine*."

We all laughed. And they got back to wrestling, and I got back to work.

They *are* fine.

I *am* a good mom.

My brand of motherhood is unique and special, and it works for our family.

Things aren't always perfectly balanced, but they're steady and good. I want to quit worrying about achieving balance anyway. It's better when I focus on whether things are fine and good.

And they *are* fine.

And we're all good.

And, actually, come to think of it . . . that feels like balance to me.

A Mama's Job
Is Never Done

EMILY GLOVER

When every day is a marathon of to-dos, should-dos, and I-needs, it can feel hard to catch your breath. You don't even cross a finish line! You just step off the course for a few hours before you start running again. The truth is, a mama's job is never done, and it's exhausting.

Your wake-up call comes in the form of a crying baby, not an alarm . . .

You feel as though you've worked a full day, but it's only breakfast . . .

If nap times magically align, you still don't do anything for yourself because you're sure someone will wake up any second . . .

There are disagreements to referee, appointments to taxi to, and meals to cater . . .

You get the kids to bed and collapse on the couch just in time to hear "Mama" echo through the house . . .

You strip the sheets and give baths and cuddle at 2:00 a.m. because someone has been sick . . .

The truth is, a mama's job is never done.

You may have imagined what motherhood would be like. You'd have the power to turn tears into giggles or turn everyday conflicts into teachable moments. But you may not have imagined just how relentless these needs can be. It isn't just *one* tantrum or conflict but a series that has to be handled along with the shoes that need to be tied, the diapers that need to be changed, and the laundry that needs to be done.

There is a special kind of beauty in this, and you won't have to look hard to see it. Each time my son says "Hold you, Mama" in that sweet toddler way of his, I swoon over this amazing little person who thinks I can solve every problem in his world.

But lately, when my son *really* wants something, he calls, "Mommyyyyy!"— stretching it to make sure I'm paying attention. Some days, it's the only name I hear, days when I feel like I'm stretched to my very limit.

The truth is, a mama's job is never done.

This life isn't as much of a choice as it is an instinct. When I hear my baby cry in the middle of the night, I don't pause to think about whether I'd rather stay in bed. I get up and nurse her, listening to the silence of night and thinking how lucky I am to hold in my arms this child, who has lived so long in my heart.

Just three years into my parenting journey, I'm already seeing how quickly our children's needs evolve. It won't be long before wiping runny noses will be replaced by shuttling kids to sports practices and then helping them pack up their bedroom before they move off to college.

In time, we all hope our children will be confident enough to solve their own problems, to be able to confide in someone else, to be in charge of making their own dreams come true. We'll feel such pride and a bit of heartache, wondering if maybe our job really *is* done.

The truth is, a mama's job is never done. And you'll be grateful for that.

The Emotional Load of Motherhood

CATHERINE DIETRICH

I see you on the playground, pushing your son on the swings. "Higher! Higher!" We don't know each other, but even as you're laughing at something he says, I can almost hear the whirring of your thoughts . . .

What should I make for dinner?

Are we behind on their shots?

Tomorrow is library day.

I really need to buy new toothbrushes.

Why isn't the baby sleeping through the night?

The emotional labor of motherhood is draining.

As soon as one problem is resolved, another pops up, and another, and another. Because, mama, every day you are the keeper of the mundane. And as each tiny, menial task piles on top of another, the load becomes heavier and heavier to carry.

As the traditional gender roles of our parents' or grandparents' generations have fallen by the wayside, marriages, partnerships, and families are, inevitably, stronger because of it. Fathers do laundry, cooking, school runs, and playdates as well as mothers do. So why does my husband sleep soundly at night while my sleepless mind races with worries? Why does the weight of the small things feel so heavy?

I'm the thinker. I'm the overthinker. I'm the worrier.

I'm the "noticer" when the toilet roll and peanut butter supply are running low. I'm the "maker" of appointments when my children's shots are due or they need haircuts. I'm the "decider" who knows what's for dinner. And I'm the "creator" of brand-new ways to get them to eat their veggies.

I'm the "reminder" to take schoolbooks, sports bags, ballet shoes, and bake sale money. I'm the "keeper" of schedules, secrets, Band-Aids, and the peace. I'm the "knower" of all my children's favorites. I'm the "instigator" of homework, chores, teeth brushing, and bedtime.

I'm the "signer" of permission slips and the "returner" of school forms. I'm the "writer" of thank-you cards, Christmas cards, birthday cards, and notes to the teacher when they need to leave early for a dentist appointment.

I'm the "tidier" of toys, the "knower" of where the Barbies go—which is *not* where the Legos go or where the dress-up things go or where the puzzles or coloring books are kept.

I'm the "planner" of playdates, birthday parties, holidays, and games. I'm the "buyer" of birthday gifts, sunscreen, formula, and new school shoes. I'm the "distributor" of snacks and treats and the "refuser" when one more treat than is reasonable is requested.

I'm the "wiper" of little bottoms, faces, tears, and spills. I'm the "soother" of ouchies, bad dreams, and arguments with best friends. I'm the cheerleader, admonisher, negotiator, and biggest fan.

> I'm the thinker.
> I'm the overthinker.
> I'm the worrier.

I am "Mom," "Mama," "Mommy," "Mother," and "Mommmmeeeeeeeee!"

And it's impossible for me *not* to be, even for a moment. Nor would I want to.

The trouble is, these millions of tiny little things are hard to track. The hours we spend thinking, worrying, planning, and noticing are impossible to quantify. The hours spent sewing on name tags, cooking meals, and trimming fingernails really can't be counted.

While my partner and I are equals, the emotional load we carry is not. A bulk of my load is invisible to everyone else but me. And we don't get a prize for this or a special reward or a quarterly bonus . . . or even a "thank you" in many situations. So what do I have to show for all of this labor?

My "payment" is the privilege to be the "entrustor" of their hearts, the "protector" of their spirits, and the "coproducer" of their dreams. And there is a gift of love in all of this noticing and nurturing. It's a gift of attention and devotion, and it's as much a gift to me as it is to those around me.

The Bedtime Dance

ASHLEY WASILENKO

The time between 5:00 p.m. and bedtime is often like a wild roller-coaster ride. As a working mom of two, I feel I need to squeeze into this three-hour window everything that I missed during the day. There's a lot to do! Dinner, playtime, bath time, reading books, tracking down stuffed animals, brushing teeth, and getting the kids off to sleep. (Oh, and the inevitable request for just *one more* story . . .)

The nighttime goes something like this:

Bath for the baby? Nope, skip that for tonight. I'm just going to be honest, tonight is not our night.

Lotion? Nope, he's crying too much, and dinner took *forever* to prepare. And we are *way* behind schedule.

Goodnight Moon? Yes, I can recite that in my sleep, in the dark, with my eyes closed. This part seems manageable.

Nursing session? Yes. But if it lasts for forty-five minutes like last night, I may nod off from exhaustion.

Most nights it feels as if I go from being consumed by the complete and utter chaos to a sense of wistful calmness in a matter of seconds.

I admire your sweet, heart-shaped lips and long curled eyelashes as you drift off to sleep. I resist the urge to kiss your *oh-so-kissable* cheeks. I don't want to wake you and undo all that I have done to get you off to sleep just for one more selfish kiss. I put you down and creep out of the room, tiptoeing around every creaky floorboard.

I'm shot, and just as I'm ready to rest my head on my fluffy pillow—*eek!*—you are up again.

Most nights, I don't mind. I want to be the one to pick you up, to make it okay, to snuggle you *just a little bit more*. The time, exhausting as it may be, goes by so fast. So, my sweet baby, I will be there during those long tiring days that somehow turn into long tiring nights. Because I know that the time when you'll fit so perfectly in my arms is fleeting, and before I know it I won't be rocking you to sleep anymore.

> Most nights it feels as if I go from being consumed by the complete and utter chaos to a sense of wistful calmness in a matter of seconds.

My oldest, a threenager, is a constant reminder of how fast it all goes. As cliché as it sounds, I blinked, and he was a big boy. A *real* kid. A nightly bubble bath has turned into a shower, which he can do mostly by himself. *Goodnight Moon* has turned into a word guessing game. Even though he's not little anymore, he still needs us for bedtime—to help him put on his pj's, to tuck him in, to sing him a song, to get him *just one more* sip of water, and to ponder life's biggest, most philosophical questions.

But soon enough (or not soon enough . . . it depends on the night), the chaos calms down and the stalling is over. They are both in bed. Sleeping. We did it.

As my husband and I find time to sit down for what feels like the first time all day, something strange happens. I miss my babies. I want to see their sweet faces again. I resist the urge to go sneak into their rooms to admire our precious boys.

I guess, at the end of the day, I'm just like my threenager. I, too, turn into a philosopher as I think back on the day. *Did they watch too much TV? Was I a good enough mom? Did I have enough patience? Did I teach them something new today? Do they know how much I love them? Am I cherishing every moment?*

The dance of bedtime has many complicated steps. Sometimes we move perfectly to the beat. But other times our rhythm is totally off. Even so, the effort is there, and our skills are getting stronger with time.

One day maybe we'll nail the choreography, maybe things will become just a little easier before the routine changes yet again. For now, we'll keep practicing. And, as I sit in the dark and silence, rocking my babe to sleep, I think of all the moms out there at the very same moment, rocking, hugging, comforting—all sharing in the sacredness of our collective bedside vigil.

I Vow to Take Care of Myself

DIANA SPALDING

I am a mama.

I grew my baby with love and energy. I went to my prenatal appointments, avoided some of the foods and drinks I loved, and touched my growing belly with amazement. I happily gave my baby everything she needed, everything I had.

I adopted my baby with love and energy. I went to every class and appointment, filled out mountains of paperwork, and waited with bated breath for the phone to ring. When they told me he was mine, I cried so hard my body shook with love.

Every day, I pour my love and energy into my children. I nurse their ailments, make their appointments, buy their clothes, clean their messes, wash their bodies, and I do it all without even thinking about it because their needs are my calling.

My days revolve around them. When I became their mother, I vowed to do everything in my power to keep my children well, safe, and thriving. I pour from my dehydrating cup to ensure that theirs are overflowing.

I love them, but I am growing weary.

When I wake up in the morning, my body hurts; at night, I don't fall asleep, I *crash* asleep. I feel my fuse growing dimmer, my temper growing stronger—and it's not fair to anyone. Somewhere along this journey, I lost myself a bit. In my effort to keep everyone else intact, I am starting to unravel at the seams.

But that changes today.

Today—and every day moving forward—I vow to do more for myself. It's not about moving people lower down on my priority list; it's about moving myself higher. It's about treating myself with the same respect I give everyone else.

I am worth it. And my family is worth it. They want me to flourish. And so, from now on, I vow to flourish.

I vow to be a source of love and energy for myself. I vow to remember that while "Mama" is my name and my heart's work, I am still a person. I vow to listen to my body and respect its messages.

> I vow to listen to my body and respect its messages.

I would never force my children to keep playing when they are tired and want to sleep—why do I force myself to keep working?

When I am tired, I will rest.

I would never deny my children healthy, energizing food when they are hungry—so why is it okay for me to be "too busy" to eat?

When I am hungry, I will eat food that nourishes my body and my soul.

I would never ignore my children's complaints or refuse to take them to the doctor—why do I feel the need to "tough it out" instead of asking for support?

When I am sick, I will carve time out of my day to seek help and heal.

I would never diminish my children's feelings or tell them they're being ridiculous—so why do I sweep my emotions under the rug and tell myself to "be stronger?"

When I am emotional, I will allow myself to experience the full range of my emotions without guilt, dismissal, or judgment.

I vow to be gentler with myself.

I vow to be kinder to myself.

I vow to offer myself love, energy, and compassion, just like I do my children.

My family is a tree—my children are the branches and I am the trunk. The life-giving nutrients make their way up the roots and to the branches through me. If I am weak or depleted, the branches won't withstand the force of the wind. But if I am rested, sturdy, and strong, the branches will reach higher and the entire tree will take in more sunlight. The branches, the trunk, and the roots will all be working together to thrive.

So I vow to take care of myself. Not because I *deserve to*, but because I *have to*. I have to for me, for my little branches, and for the whole forest of mamas around me.

The Gift of Attention

COURTNEY ROCHOWICZ

Sitting at my desk now, I turn my head and look down our hallway to see the back of my son's soft, fuzzy, eleven-month-old head, his chubby legs swinging freely in his highchair. Craning his neck, he's following his dad's every move with rapt attention.

I don't want to miss a moment with my son, and of course, I will.

My heart tells me to shut my laptop. There's nothing more pressing than snuggling with my son as he rests his head on my shoulder. Yet *my* head is full of deadlines, due dates, and meetings that this heart of mine doesn't always want to acknowledge.

Do you know this tug? The ceaseless battle between heart and head, the struggle of mom versus all of the other versions of ourselves—all of the many hats we wear?

I don't want to miss a moment—but I want to finish the exciting project I am responsible for at work. And I need space and quiet to do so.

I don't want to miss a moment—but I desperately want to go out to dinner with my husband and have a focused conversation.

I don't want to miss a moment—but I want to catch up with my girl-friends over drinks without guilt hanging over my head.

I don't want to miss a moment—but I want to make it to yoga on time so I can give myself an hour to check in with how I am feeling and doing.

I don't want to miss a moment—but I want to fold the laundry and put the toys away without tiny (albeit cute) hands making a mess of the tasks I just completed.

I don't want to miss a moment—but I know I have to stay centered to resist the urge to fill all my free time with screen time, podcasts, or phone calls.

The pull of this life can be a real struggle. Some days I feel like I can't possibly be everything to everyone. I can't manage everything I need to. Some days, honestly, the pull is just too much.

What I'm realizing now is that being a mother is not about balance. It's about boundaries. It's about attention. It's about choosing to dedicate my time, energy, and focus to whatever is in front of me at any given point throughout my day.

But the distractions steal some of the joy.

Because attention is love. Presence is love. Listening is love. Being seen is love.

There will always be *something* that begs for my attention. Is it tempting to check my email while I'm building a tower of blocks with my son? Yes. Is it tempting to make a phone call while at the park with my family? Yes. Is it tempting to respond to the text from my mom while my husband is telling me about his day? Yes.

But the distractions steal some of the joy.

There might *never* be a perfect equilibrium in my days, and fighting for it is exhausting and maddening. Instead, I try to create boundaries to protect me from anything that wants to interfere with what I'm doing in the present moment.

As a multitasking parent, I may not always be a paragon of efficiency every second, but I am getting better at paying attention to the things that fill my heart *and* head with energy and love. The things I'm not passionate about don't take up as much space as they used to.

Motherhood has shown me what's important in life. I know what I want to dedicate my time to.

My everyday challenge now is to make sure the important things get the important attention they deserve.

practice
WELLNESS CHECKLIST

ERIN LEYBA

We are constantly taking good care of those around us—our kids, our partners, our friends—and it's important that we take care of ourselves too.

While motherhood can be chaotic and exhausting, making your personal wellness and happiness a priority can help you fill your cup so you can stay balanced and joyful—and have more to give.

To help support your self-care efforts, here's a list of practical reminders for ways to make sure you're giving yourself the attention you deserve:

- Drink enough water. Aim for six to eight glasses a day, more if you're nursing.

- Take a few minutes to stretch your neck, back, arms, and legs.

- Text a friend just to say hi.

- Do something funny that will make your child laugh.

- Take a walk, even if it's just around the block.

- Each day make a list of three things you're grateful for.

- Play a song (or a few) that will boost your mood or remind you of a special time in your life.

- Eat a nourishing meal or snack.

- Identify three things you're looking forward to in the next month or two.

- Play with your child side-by-side on the floor for fifteen minutes, following their lead.

- Do a one-minute meditation by closing your eyes and focusing on your breath.

- Leave a kind comment (not just a "like") on someone's Instagram post.

- Hug someone warmly.

- Open a window or light a candle.

- Plan a date night with your partner.

- Take an electronics break after 9:00 p.m.

- Bring mindfulness to one tedious chore and really focus on the experience of *doing*.

- Go outside. Feel the earth beneath your feet. Notice the sky. Take three deep breaths.

- Sit down and put your feet up for ten minutes.

- Catch your child doing something good by saying, "I see you [fill in the blank, such as "being so nice to your brother"]."

- Put a favorite lotion on your hands and face.

- Remind yourself that though parenting is often incredible, it can also be hard and exhausting. And it's okay to think that.

- Declutter your to-do list by completing one task that will lower your stress level.

- Reflect on one way you're an especially good parent. Write it down.

- Greet someone new and strike up a friendly conversation.

- Get yourself in bed by 9:00 p.m. at least one night this week.

- Remind yourself: You are awesome.

journal QUESTIONS

- What experiences deplete your energy most during the day? What could you do to change this or make it a little bit better?

- What do you need help with most? Can your partner or a friend help in this area?

- What do you do that is solely for you and you only?

Love

In family life, love is the oil that eases friction, the cement
that binds closer together, and the music that brings harmony.
EVA BURROWS

INTRODUCTION

LIZ TENETY

Commitment—whether through a marriage ceremony or another
vow—bonds a couple together. But a baby turns you from two people into
a family—forever.

As a family, you get to navigate tradition, expectation, hopes, dreams,
and disappointment—together. As a family, you get to make a life full of
joy and meaning by one another's sides. And you have the opportunity to
write a new story for this new generation.

**There's no doubt that riding this wave of parenthood with each
other is full of the highest highs and some of the lowest lows.**

The ecstatic feeling of watching your partner hold the newborn baby
you made together. The deep angst when you feel you're invisible to the one
you love. The fact that some of the biggest joys can come from the simplest
moments, and the largest fights can emerge from the smallest tasks (here's
to the great fight over who packed the diaper bag).

Parenthood has it all.

And I have felt it all too.

But here's the good news: There is no one script for how to do this. Your
marriage or partnership doesn't have to be the same as anyone else's.
Your home can be whatever you define it to be. Your work-life balance
can be determined according to your needs. Your division of duties can be

something you two decide, together. And once decided, they can change to meet the needs of each season too.

The many challenges of love and parenthood don't have to become insurmountable hardships. They can be awe-inspiring, hilarious, and profound. Most of all, they present an opportunity to create the life you've imagined, to craft the relationship you need, and to charge into the future, defining as a couple what a happy home looks like to you.

It all requires empathy. Trust. Commitment. Vulnerability. Forgiveness. It *is* a lot. But this is what "for better or worse" is all about.

This is your relationship. Your family. Your home. What do you want your story to be?

P.S. At the end of this section is a tool for you to use to create a family manifesto with your partner. This will help you envision the type of culture you want to create in your home and will hold you accountable in keeping to your core values—as a team.

This Is Us

ALICIA KESWANI

The weeks after our daughter was born came with a whirlwind of change that knocked the wind right out of me. I missed my pre-baby life and I was racked with guilt because of it. It's taken over a year, but I'm finally able to understand why that season felt so . . . clunky: We didn't feel like a *family* yet.

Before Ella was born, we were a couple who loved everything, from a spontaneous weekend trip to running errands to dreaming about the future together. But immediately following Ella's birth, we no longer felt like a couple. It was more like two adults playing a 24/7 tag-team game of caring for our precious baby while the other got some sleep.

In my rawest moments, I felt threatened that our marriage would dissolve into an endless list of things to do, chores to complete, and bills to pay. Bye-bye, spontaneous life of adventure and fun. See you later, weekend brunch. Bye-bye, best friend and love of my life. See you when we retire.

My breaking point came on a Saturday morning when I said goodbye to my husband as he left for the grocery store.

Going to the store was something we did together before the baby. Now it was one more thing among many things that completely changed. It became a chore.

Any veteran parent could recognize that we were in the throes of the fourth trimester. Baby blues, mama's recovery, and zero sleep for everyone makes your heart raw and vulnerable at depths you didn't know were possible. Your emotions run wild and you find yourself ugly crying about the strangest things.

My husband had cheered me on as my body adapted and grew with our daughter. Now both of us were being shaped into parents. It's a shaping of the soul, sweet and difficult, one that stretches you to the brink only to find you have more strength than you ever imagined.

And make no mistake — it *is* a transformation.

Before I became a mother, I thought it happened as easily as flipping on a light switch. Poof, hello mama! Poof, hello daddy! In retrospect, it seems laughable. How can the deep and holy calling of parenthood happen with the flick of a switch? How can a marriage of two souls shift to become the foundation for a new life? As with many beautiful things in life, these changes happen over time with mistakes and learning, tears and laughter.

As we watched the mommy and daddy emerge within one another, it brought a new depth of love and appreciation to our marriage.

This is the
new Us.

This is the *new* Us.

The other Saturday, we woke up early, made coffee, and let Ella stay in her pajamas while we piled onto the couch, chatting about our week. Then we stuck her in the stroller and walked two blocks to the grocery store. Ella cooed and watched us as we picked out produce, bread, and eggs. She insisted on helping carry the load, so she held onto one of her new food pouches.

As we went in and out of chatting with each other while baby talking to Ella, my husband paused, looked at me with a smile, and said, "Can you believe it? This is our family."

I write this knowing a family is an ever-evolving thing. We will change and remold ourselves when each challenge comes along. The greatest victory of all was learning that there is no finish line, no way to check all the boxes.

Life isn't a light switch, it's a potter's wheel—one that will shape what we know about *us* again and again and again.

The Small Things
Are the Big Things

EMILY GLOVER

To my love,

So often during our busy days, the little phrase of "thank you" is thrown around without restraint. *Thank you* for taking out the trash. *Thank you* for reminding me you're the one picking our son up from childcare. *Thank you* for granting my request for ten minutes of alone time.

Of course, there's nothing wrong with that. There's no cost attached to "thank you"—but a great one that comes in its absence.

"Thank you" often goes without saying, when it actually deserves to be said the most . . .

Like those times when you do things without asking. Without expectation. Without need for notice. Because I still do notice. And, my love, thank you . . . for quietly walking with our son outside to play after you notice I've fallen asleep on the couch . . . for volunteering for more hours at work after you saw me anxiously checking the bank account following unexpected expenses . . . for modeling how to balance interests and responsibilities—and then empowering me to do the same.

Thank you for never accusing me of being hormonal, even though that's probably what caused my irrational breakdown over our toddler's misplaced hat that I *just loved so much* during my first trimester with baby number two . . . for telling me I'm beautiful, even when it's 7:00 a.m. and that's *probably* spit-up on my robe . . . for encouraging me to buy a new outfit for myself "because you don't buy many clothes for yourself," even though you would never ask for something in exchange.

Thank you for doing the dishes that were sitting in the sink overnight first thing in the morning, when I'm still too groggy to notice they were ever left behind. Thank you for wrestling with our son one minute and then joyfully reading him a fairytale the next.

Most of all, thank you for doing this life with me as we figure out just how much the better in "for better or worse" can be when we're in it together.

Raising Our Kids Together, Separately

SARA GOLDSTEIN

A Google search of "will divorce . . ." autopopulates with ". . . ruin my child" and provides almost a million results. Clearly, choosing to separate isn't a decision *anyone* takes lightly, especially when kids are involved. However, for many families, it's their reality.

My kids were four and ten when their dad and I split. After a twelve-year run, we'd grown apart. It was sad. It was hard. And when I moved a few miles down the road out of the sweet little home we'd created together, I wondered how I'd ever prove to all three of them that this uncharted, bramble-covered path was the right one to take.

This path, with two homes, goodnight FaceTimes instead of goodnight kisses, and split holidays. This path, so completely different than the ones our friends and family were traveling down. This path, which at first glance divided "all" and "nothing" but upon closer inspection paved a flourishing way between the two.

Our path hasn't been without its bumps, but with consistency key and our children at the forefront of the cause, we're finding our way as we go. And nearly two years later, we've found a new "normal" that includes step-parents, stepdogs—and simply trying our best.

Many people equate divorce with failure—a failed attempt at bringing to life the vision of the future you once shared, a failure to keep a promise. But evaluating the success of a relationship based on how long it lasts *hardly* seems fair. The time frame alone doesn't account for the little victories and lessons learned. In this "failed" relationship, we learned and grew so much, ultimately evolving into better versions of ourselves along the way. Our lives, way different looking now than we thought they'd be twelve years ago, are still full of love because of this family we have created together. Raising our children together—separately—is possible because, ultimately, we have stuck to the plan: choosing to put them first.

We set rules together.

Structure and consistency help everyone thrive, so parallel expectations and rules are key—no matter where our kids' mornings start. We stay in close communication about behavioral challenges and new attitudes and shift rules accordingly, together—we don't micromanage.

We respect each other.

No matter what's going on, I don't let my feelings about my ex complicate my kids' view of him or contribute to an unnecessary rift between them. Those feelings of frustration/irritation/heartbreak are mine, not theirs.

We don't feel pressured to turn into the fun concierge.

Since I'm not with my kids *all* the time, it's easy to feel like I need to make up for it somehow when we are together. But I don't. We let life carry on as ordinarily as usual. We read books, ride bikes, I take time for myself. Our kids need that "regular life" as much as ever.

We work together as a team.

If there's something important the other parent needs to know, we deliver the message ourselves—we don't use our kids as messengers.

And when possible, we spend time all together. Even if it's uncomfortable or awkward, putting differences aside for a birthday celebration speaks volumes to our kids.

We hold strong to our resolve. Although time doesn't heal all wounds, it's certainly a nice salve.

No, things will never be the same. But there's comfort in knowing that as time goes by, I recalibrate. The waves of emotion that used to blindside me as the door closed behind my kids have become less intense. The heart-clutching anxiety that my kids are going to suffer stops waking me up in the middle of the night (or at least less often).

We've found a steadiness on this uncharted path.

Like so many of the relationships that we build in the course of a well-lived lifetime, marriages often grow apart. The inevitability of a happily-ever-after together eventually doesn't feel quite so inevitable anymore. Many relationships don't stay the same over time—friendships evolve, siblings move away, jobs and bosses change. But we can't measure, in terms of time, the valuable lessons we've learned from them.

And while my own marriage didn't last as long as either of us had envisioned, we built a life filled with laughter, inside jokes, and the creation of two of the most incredible people I could ever have imagined. And we continue to navigate this new road together, separately.

We don't feel pressured to turn into the fun concierge.

Choosing Each Other Again and Again

COLLEEN TEMPLE

Our love story is fairly typical. We met in college, started dating senior year, survived long distance for a year after graduation, got engaged, moved in together, got married, and had our first child about a year and a half after we said "I do."

But just because it may seem typical doesn't mean it's always easy. Ten years after we started dating, five of them married, we now have three children, a mortgage, bills, jobs, stress, and happiness. Lots of adult things, but not always lots of romantic things.

On most days, our love looks like big hugs from little humans covered in peanut butter . . . like two exhausted parents sitting next to each other binge-watching *just one more* episode . . . like everyday frustrations and bits of encouragement.

I'm noticing, more and more every day, that our commitment to each other is woven into our every day. It's in the small things *and* the big things. The quiet things and the boisterous things. It's simple and special. Sweet and proud.

Most importantly, I think our love is a choice.

Sometimes it takes effort—to schedule a babysitter, to muster up enough energy to go out on a date, to say "I'm sorry" with grace and forgiveness. It's a love that requires the patience of waiting to be ready to have sex again after the baby. And a love that requires time to connect at the end of a long day. Every day that we wake up is a day we choose to put in the work—it's a day that we choose each other.

I see my husband's commitment when he wakes up at 3:00 a.m. to calm our crying kiddo—even though he has to get ready for work in two hours. I show mine when I am on my third nursing session of the night and it's not even 3:00 a.m. yet. I feel our commitment to each other with every family adventure we go on together. I know our commitment is strong when he accepts my apology or when each of us is the only person the other would want to be with upon receiving bad news. I watch our commitment in action when he drops the argument or when I bite my tongue and let him get the last word in—even when I may want to say more.

This choice is one we make again and again (and again).

Our marriage is strong because we work on it, not because we pretend we're perfect and that we're so in love that we can look forward to decades of success. Teamwork (*and* love) is what will get us through. Because on the happiest days, love is our choice. And on our toughest days? We choose love then too. In the big moments, the small moments—and everything in between—love is there.

Our love may be many things, but it's not a burden. While it definitely requires effort and attention, it's something that comes as naturally to me as breathing.

So, yes, love is a choice. But choosing to love this man every day? Well, that's an easy one.

Let's Talk About Sex (After Baby)

RASCHAEL ASH

Anything under "things to do for myself" has fallen to the bottom of my to-do list since the birth of my second child: buying clothes, going to the dentist, getting a mani-pedi (please don't look at my feet)—and at the bottom of that list, way down near "get an eye exam," is my sex life.

With my firstborn, it didn't take us nearly as long to get back into the swing of things. I'd read that parenting was synonymous with a lack of sex, but I didn't buy it. When I gave birth for the first time four years ago, I already had a stepchild who was five, and I thought, *What's the problem? We don't have trouble finding time for sex.*

I didn't understand.

So naïve of me.

Now that I have a baby, a four-year-old, and a nine-year-old, it's a whole other ball game. No, actually, it's a whole different sport. And I often feel like I don't know how to play the game.

By the end of a full day with two little kids, plus the before- and after-school shuffle with suppertime, bath time, and bedtime routines added in, the last thing on my mind is romance.

Throughout my days, there's a lot of touching from tiny toddler hands.

In fact, I'm pretty sure my baby has decided that my left breast belongs to her. She tries to take it with her any which way she goes. (Here's hoping the "old girl" bounces back to center position and recovers from the trauma.) Once the kids are finally in bed, some days the last thing I want is someone else touching me. (Unless it's a masseuse specializing in deep tissue massage. Otherwise, back up off me.)

Adjusting to my postpartum body has also been a challenge. I know my body is beautiful and my partner tells me so, but being positive about it is a work in progress.

It has nothing to do with my partner and everything to do with the state of our lives. I am still drawn to him physically and sexually, especially when he's playing with our children or washing the dishes (hint, hint). But at the end of the day, many things are weighing me down, making it almost impossible to get in the mood. And sometimes this mama just needs some sleep.

I know my partner misses the embraces I used to give him when he came home. Instead, it's a quick hug from me and I direct the kids toward him. I love him beyond measure, but I love me too, and at this time in our lives I desperately need fifteen minutes of peace and quiet when he walks through that door.

The truth is . . . we need one another more than ever.

It's as if, in order to give myself to him, I need to give myself something else first: the chance to just be alone.

Sometimes it seems there are many obstacles in the way of romance. There have been times when we're looking forward to alone time, but then our baby wakes up crying because of a bad dream or a child needs help NOW! There have even been times we have had to cancel our sitter because someone was sick, so there goes date night. Romance in this stage of life doesn't always go according to plan. But we keep trying because we know how important our time together is, so we pencil it in—sex included.

When we first met and were falling in love, neither of us thought we'd have to check our calendars to find the best time to squeeze in romantic time together. While it may sound boring, for us, it's a necessity. We're doing what we need to do to make each other a priority, and honestly, there's romance in that kind of devotion.

I recognize that this is temporary. It's a fleeting era of chaos. Eventually, the busyness will calm down and we'll have more time for each other again. Until then, I'm fine with our definition of romance in this season: a text from my partner telling me he's taking the kids to the park. Without me.

Maybe right now, romance is watching our partners do the dishes while we relax. Maybe it's holding hands on the couch after a long day. Maybe it's fitting sex in during nap time or giving one another massages before bed. Although our romance looks different, the ways it's expressed have so much more depth and breadth and meaning than before.

The truth is, while the endless needs of parenthood can make us feel touched out and beyond tired, we need one another more than ever.

For us, scheduling sex isn't something to feel bad about. Instead, it's a sign of our fierce commitment to each other in this busy season. This love is alive, well, and worthy of celebration. It's a love worth scheduling.

Love Is Love
and It Prevails

AMBER LEVENTRY

Falling in love with each other twenty years ago wasn't meant to happen. Friends, family, and society weren't supportive of our same-sex relationship. But finding a home within each other's soul was no mistake. That's why when my partner's biological clock started ticking so loudly it couldn't be ignored, it was time to plan. And our decisions were very intentional.

Nothing is an accident when it comes to same-sex family building.

We knew how babies were conceived. But how would *we* conceive a baby? We went to LGBTQ-friendly doctors and lawyers. We went to online sperm banks. We went to the books.

The first book my partner and I purchased was *Taking Charge of Your Fertility* by Toni Weschler, MPH. We learned about ovulation cycles, basal body temperature, and other tips for baby-making success. However, unlike other couples, we needed sperm.

After shopping for the best anonymous sperm donor—one who resembled me in looks and personality (based on answers to surveys and essay questions)—doctors at a fertility clinic inseminated my partner through intrauterine insemination.

Although I didn't biologically help create our children, I felt as much like a parent as anyone else does because of the love I poured into the process.

Some families need to gather different pieces to puzzle together a family. I was reminded of this when reading pregnancy and parenting books. It was hard to relate to the naming conventions. I wasn't the pregnant woman or the father-to-be. I was the nonbiological mother-to-be. And since they don't write about this role in the "expecting" books, I felt left out of the conversation.

I realize I'm not the only one left out of these conversations.

Our culture's standard recipe for family building remains very homogenous— yet the reality is so diverse. If we look at what makes a family, it's love. And that love looks like sacrifice, determination, and often creativity, regardless of your gender or sexual preference.

It's love that finds a way to win, despite what seems like insurmountable obstacles in its way. It's love that discovers a deeper selflessness than you ever knew you had. It's love that swells when you gaze at your partner holding your child.

Love is a feeling, a force, a strength, a superpower. You can't quite touch it, but love is the most real thing there is.

This love looks like single women jumping through hoops and spending a lot of money to find an adoption agency able to help them bring a child into their lives. It looks like a longtime couple's years of infertility, IVF treatments, and heartbreaking miscarriages too. It can look like a gender-nonconforming person working creatively with their partner and doctor to make a baby. It can even look like an unplanned pregnancy that a woman decides to embrace, changing the course of her life forever. This love is where babies come from.

But our culture still needs to catch up to our reality.

As my partner and I were trying to have a baby, I read the parenting and baby books, mentally changing the words from "father" and "husband" to "second mother" and "partner." I spoke up when our birth class instructor insisted on using the term "daddy" instead of "partner." Perhaps you, too, need to tweak words or change frameworks to better reflect your reality.

Parenthood is a universal idea—but sometimes we need to redefine the term to fit us.

This happens to other parents too. Single mothers, adoptive mothers, mothers who work outside of the home, mothers who are stay-at-home moms, men who are stay-at-home dads, and interracial families all work within a culture that often lacks the language to include them.

The thing is, families don't look the same. Sometimes they have two moms or two dads. Sometimes they have one mom and one dad. Sometimes they have only one mom *or* dad. At the core, though, we all have something in common—love.

My cells did not create my son and two daughters; my children did not grow from anything tangible I possess. But the connection I feel to them and the stories we are writing by living in the margins are as true and as real as if we did share DNA.

It's not always easy being in the minority, living in the heteronormative majority. As a same-sex couple raising three kids, we don't fit the mold of other families at the park, the library, or the school dance. Our two-mom family is accepted and respected, and we fit in, but situations and experiences don't always fit *us*—so we adjust.

You will adjust too. Love will prevail.

That's the most surprising and unplanned thing about love. Despite friends, family, and society telling us that our love is wrong, we love anyway. We constantly walk around in a world that doesn't always fit our needs and wants, but we walk anyway.

I suspect love is also your family's foundation. So let's build families based on love—wholehearted, big love. Let's be brave and do what's best for our families. Let's be confident in our choices. And let's allow our love to propel us forward into a future where the universal things in life fit everyone, not just some.

Let's Not Wait to Make Time for Us

COLLEEN TEMPLE

My darling, I want to tell you . . .

One day we're going to wake up and our kiddos will be adults. Can you imagine those perfect little bodies turning into adult-size bodies with jobs and big responsibilities? I want them to, of course. But still, it's a little trippy thinking about what they'll be like.

Our babies are going to move out and have lives of their own. They're going to create families. Their families will become priority number one, and we'll move gracefully down the list. It'll be hard to let go, I'm sure. Maybe even heartbreaking. Sometimes I stay awake at night wondering if they're going to ask to go to college five hours (or more!) away from us—like I did to my parents.

Sometimes I think about life with you when they're grown.

We're going to have lots of uninterrupted time together again. We can travel, explore, and go on adventures of a new kind. We can try that fancy restaurant on a whim without finding a babysitter. Or maybe we'll invite our grown children to join us for that nice dinner and we'll enjoy adult conversation together. The days when we'd attempt to go out to dinner with our little ones will feel like a lifetime ago.

We'll wake up and fall asleep together. It'll be quiet in our house. No more loud singing of *The Little Mermaid* soundtrack, no more fighting over toys, no more giggles when we make funny faces. We can have all the uninterrupted conversation we want. No topic will be too deep, no good debate will take up too much time.

We're going to have all of this when our kids are grown, but why wait?

Sure, life is busy now. And loud. And it takes more organization and planning and patience. But we can't put connecting on hold. We can't put meaningful conversation on hold. We can't put touching on hold.

Our love should be lived to the max. Every. Single. Day. The reality is, no one knows when their time is up. Life is here. It's happening now. My love for you is so deep and so much a part of me. I want to celebrate that now—not later.

> Our love should be lived to the max. Every. Single. Day.

Connecting with you can't wait until retirement, so let's do it now.

Let's not answer every single request at the drop of a dime, especially when we're talking about something important. Let's continue our conversation and ask our kiddo to wait a few minutes until mommy and daddy are done.

Let's embrace the noise together even as we wonder how these little creatures can make such loud noises. I want to memorize our three-year-old's singing voice. (I mean, no one sings "Part of Your World" better than her.) I want to tattoo our sixteen-month-old's giggles into my long-term memory. I want to take mental pictures of you playing—loud, uninhibitedly playing—with our kids and tuck them away in a safe place.

Let's go on family adventures and dates.

I know our trips aren't going to be perfect and may stray far from the original plan. Still, let's be open-minded. Let's show our children new people, places, and communities to instill a sense of wonder in them. This will be my greatest adventure with you.

Let's put dating in our budget. We'll try that new restaurant or just sit quietly together over a cup of coffee. It doesn't have to cost a ton of money—a few minutes together in the park on a nice day could be exactly what we need.

The point is, I love you now, I'll love you when we retire, and I'll love you every second in between. But we're here in the wild-wonderful stage of parenting young children together, and I see you—an incredible father but also the sexy, intelligent, fun husband I fell in love with.

So let's love each other now. Because I don't want to wait.

practice
FAMILY MANIFESTO

REBECCA EANES

Happy, peaceful, positive families are intentionally and thoughtfully forged in the ordinary choices we make each day. The routines and traditions we create, the ways we communicate and interact, the values we live by, and the rules we uphold all serve to define what family means to us.

The culture we create in our home is the world our children grow up in. It shapes their views about themselves and others—about belonging and acceptance and, most importantly, about love. It provides a haven from all that's *out there*—a place to settle in and exhale.

A family manifesto is a tool to purposefully define what family means to you put in a form you can all see, touch, and read.

This manifesto outlines your goals, values, beliefs, and intentions. It will be your family's legacy. A great manifesto will motivate you and your partner to model the core values you want your family to uphold and will encourage you to be your best selves.

When your family's purpose becomes clear, it's easier to make decisions that are in line with that purpose. You can even use the manifesto as a positive teaching tool for your children, reminding you to guide them in a way you and your partner mutually agreed upon.

To create this manifesto, begin by having a discussion with your partner.

Talk about the family culture you want to create together. What is most important to you? What values and beliefs do you want to pass down? What do you want to avoid? What are your dreams and goals? This will help you both organize your thoughts and have a clearer idea of what you want to include.

It's helpful to have a starting point, so start with a list of values. Your family values might include gratitude, acceptance, gentleness, and compassion. Or perhaps you lean more toward adventure, practice, ambition, and courage. Write down all of the values you discuss to nail down what's most important.

Compile all of these ideas, and once you have a comprehensive list of values, beliefs, and goals, make it official and write it down. Then place it somewhere visible and accessible.

Keep your manifesto alive by reading it together regularly.

Your manifesto can serve as a great reminder of the type of family you're shaping. It can also be a wonderful tool for connecting with each other. As your family grows and your children age, you may want to reevaluate your manifesto. Eventually, you can include your children in conversations about this—explaining all that it means and represents—uniting your family in your common values and beliefs.

Here are some questions to discuss with your partner to get started:

- What kind of family do we want to be?

- What kind of atmosphere do we want in our home?

- How do we want members of our family to feel?

- What values will we uphold?

- What traditions are important to us?

- How do we have fun in this family?

- What memories do we want our children to be able to look back upon?

- What quotes inspire us?

journal QUESTIONS

- In which moments do you feel most (and least) connected as a couple?

- What are your favorite traits in your partner that you now see reflected in your child(ren)?

- How does your life now reflect or differ from the vision you once had for life with a family?

- If you could look back and offer your pre-parent self one piece of advice, what would it be?

Village

Mama, you are many good + beautiful things. But you are no village.
ALICIA KESWANI

INTRODUCTION

JILL KOZIOL

I'm a strong and independent woman, and being competent and capable is part of my personal identity. But parenthood isn't like any other aspect of life.

It's the one place where you *have* to surrender *some* control and be open to help.

This motherhood thing was not meant to be done by ourselves alone. We were meant to be surrounded by a village. We deserve a village.

Why? Because motherhood is hard. It's beautiful and it's glorious, but it's oh-so-hard. And as women, we know intuitively that kindness and friendship can make most anything lighter to carry. Why, then, do we find it so hard, as mothers, to accept help? Why are we so quick to offer a hand but see it as a failure to accept one?

For me, because my personal identity is being competent and capable, I didn't know how to reconcile that with all the demands of new motherhood.

I fought hard to not *need* help, and, in the process, I made things much harder on myself and my family.

But here's the thing—people *want* to help. They mean it when they offer it. And it doesn't have to be a power struggle. In fact, it shouldn't be. I've realized that by *not* accepting help, or by imposing my own judgment on it, I'm effectively imposing judgment on the person who has offered to help too.

It took me miscarrying twins between my daughters' births for me to realize that there was no shame, but rather a new sense of power, in accepting help. The power of my village.

In the dark days during and following the miscarriage, I discovered that our eight-month-old daughter's nanny was more than a nanny; she was a part of my village, a part of our family. I discovered that my neighbor would drop everything to hold my hand while I cried over tea and test results. I discovered that my mother would answer my call, *always*, and that I could feel her love across the country.

I discovered that I had a virtual village spread across message boards and social media feeds, lifting me up and helping me to see that I wasn't alone in this. I had found my village.

Since those days, my village has grown and evolved. It doesn't look the same as it first did.

It's changing with each new chapter of motherhood I enter. Yet it's always there, as long as I'm willing to see it, to be open to it.

We're all in this together, and no matter what your village looks like, trust me: Life—and motherhood—are *so* much better with it.

P.S. At the end of this section is a practice to assist you in building your village— that is, identifying and assembling your community. This practice is followed by a journal reflection exercise to ground you and remind you that asking for and needing help is normal and necessary. Even in the toughest moments, taking note of all the people who love and support you will help you find peace and purpose.

Be That Mom You Wish to See In the World

ANNE-MARIE GAMBELIN

There's nothing like motherhood to make you feel incredibly empowered one day and vulnerable and fragile the next. Some days you are Superwoman-Mama-Awesome—puffed up with confidence and calm—and feel like you can do it all. Bring it on.

Other days it seems overwhelming. All you want to do is stay home and avoid anything that could reinforce that you are doing it wrong or that you aren't doing enough—that *you are* not enough.

We have all been on both sides, and we know how it feels. We know when we see a mama struggling.

We see it in her eyes . . . a furtive glance locking us out. We see it in her face . . . a grimace instead of a quick smile, a furrowed brow instead of anticipation. We see it in her posture . . . a little bent, hunching in an attempt to protect a raw heart. Sometimes we even see it in her hair. (You know what I mean.)

When we see a fellow mama in that place, we need to remember to step up, step in, step out of our comfort zone . . . and be *that* mom.

For the mom who is feeling like she's not enough . . . be *that* mom who offers an encouraging word, letting her know she's doing just fine.

For the mom who is needing comfort from a hard day . . . be *that* mom who stands up for her, extends a hand, and offers a gentle word to assure her she's not alone.

For the mom who is new, shy, or lonely and seeking friends . . . be *that* mom who makes the phone call, walks across the room or parking lot, and extends a smile and a welcome for one more.

For the mom who is struggling to figure it all out . . . be *that* mom who drops off a meal and a new resource to check out, giving her hope and a break.

Some days it's hard to dig deeper and find the resolve needed to embrace the unexpected or unfamiliar.

Anything can throw you off balance and into that murky swamp of stress, anxiety, and uncertainty. Sometimes it's just because you're new. Maybe you aren't *in* with the new mommy-and-me group, and that feels awkward and lonely.

Other times it's because you're *so* tired. You've been up too many nights in a row at the mercy of a virus that has set upon each family member, leaving you on the ropes and trying your best to get back in the ring. Self-care has taken a back seat in the mom-van of life, and your gas tank is empty.

All of us have had our share of both kinds of days. We know the feeling of satisfaction and empowerment when we're in our lane. On the days that don't feel so good, we know what it feels like to have to carry on.

Everyone needs support, to be noticed, and to have someone throw us a line when we're drowning.

We've all been there. So be *that* mom.

Be a role model, not only for your kids, but for the other moms. Be *that* mom who makes the effort and has the courage to do the right thing, even when it's hard. What you give will be returned to you tenfold.

Be easy on each other and make it easy *for* each other because it's rarely easy, what we're doing. We all watch each other, we all know these complex feelings of motherhood—so let's all help each other . . . and be *that* mom.

Mom—You Made It Look Easy

EMILY GLOVER

Dear Mom,

As I was growing up, I didn't stop to think about how you did it all. You made sure our needs were met. You occasionally managed to carve out some time for yourself. You didn't complain—at least in front of us. And you loved, loved, *loved* us.

Even though you never claimed to be doing it perfectly, you seemed to be doing it effortlessly. Only now that I'm following in your footsteps with two little ones of my own, I'm looking back on my childhood through a new lens and realizing it wasn't as easy as you made it look. Not even close.

So, let me just start with this: I'm sorry I took for granted all the things that made my childhood magical and all the ways you were the magician.

Those annual family vacations up to the beach house, the "adventures" we would take on the neighborhood trails, and the happy Christmas mornings and birthday surprises didn't just come together out of thin air. *You* were the one who helped fill our childhoods with wonder.

Now that I'm the magic maker in my children's lives, I'm realizing just how much work goes on behind the curtain.

Behind each family vacation is a late, frantic night of packing everything (hopefully) we'll need. Behind each "spontaneous" hike is an urgent need to go somewhere, *anywhere* outside of the house for a while. And behind each Christmas morning or birthday surprise are hours spent searching and scheming for all the ways to make them memorable.

No, our days weren't always perfect growing up. But if you worry because you "didn't do it perfectly," know that you *were* perfect when it came to the things that mattered.

I've been asking myself how you did it, day after day, no matter whether you were sad or exhausted or overwhelmed. So I decided to actually ask you—and wouldn't you know it? You said you were trying to emulate your own mom all along. When she was raising you and your seven siblings, she didn't get hung up on being right all the time. Her goal was to support you in whatever you seemed confident enough to do.

Perhaps "seeming confident" is what motherhood is all about. Just like a magician, you must have put on a lot of showmanship each time you convinced us pizza for dinner was an *amazing treat* or made it feel like a big adventure for us to hang out with Dad at the office. Was there a little sleight of hand in play? Yes! But these were some of the most magical moments of all.

You filled our home with joy on the ordinary days, which made for such an extraordinary childhood.

While I may criticize myself some days when I feel like I'm failing to live up to the standard you set, I'm trying to think of my kids' perspectives: I may see putting sprinkles on my toddler's yogurt (so he will eat *something*) as a lowering of my standards, but he just may see it as the best breakfast ever.

In these moments, not only do I remember how magical *my* childhood was, but I realize how your confidence and influence is making my motherhood magical too.

Love,
Your daughter

Thank Goodness for Grandparents

COLLEEN TEMPLE

Grandparents are adventurers and wish granters. They're wise sounding boards and infinite pools of knowledge. They're helpful, they're supportive—and they love their grandchildren as if they were their own.

My children are lucky to have the grandparents they do. Quite honestly, we couldn't do this wild roller coaster that is parenthood without them. They watch our kids, they believe in our dreams, and they tell us we're doing a good job. (What more can you ask for?)

They're always in our family's corner—cheering us on and providing SO much support—and for that I want to say *thank you*.

To the Nanas who sit and paint with our kiddos for hours on end while making them laugh hysterically—*thank you*. (And sorry for the mess!)

To the Papas who always bring a fun, thoughtful treat that makes our children's faces light up immediately—*thank you*.

To the Grandmas who make the best chicken soup in the world (and always enough to freeze for another time!)—*thank you*.

To the Grandpas who get down on the floor with our children and play with them till the cows come home—*thank you*.

To the Mimis who tell the best, most elaborate, enthusiastic stories that our little ones are absolutely enchanted by—*thank you.*

To the Grand-pères who fish and hike and bike and dig with our kids—*thank you.*

To the Omas who have been in the delivery room with us rubbing our backs and wiping our foreheads with a cloth—*thank you.*

To the Opas who change diapers and feed our babies and wipe noses and patch up boo-boos—*thank you.*

To the Mormors who watch our children so we can go to work without worrying about the care and comfort of our precious babies—*thank you.*

To the Bedstefars who, without fail, always put money into a college savings account for their grandchildren every month—*thank you.*

To the Grammies who rock our babies to sleep so we can have a break or take a shower—*thank you.*

> For now,
> I will shout
> from the rooftops
> how much
> I love them.

To the Pop-Pops who teach our children valuable life lessons on everything from saving money to working hard and being kind—*thank you.*

To the Babas who know *just* what to say and when to say it (to us, and to the kids)—*thank you.*

To the Gigis who give THE best hugs—*thank you.*

To the Yayas who buy stylish *and* practical clothes (in the right sizes!) and new sneakers whenever the kids need them—*thank you.*

To the Pappoús who do school pickups for us—*thank you.*

To the Mawmaws and Pawpaws who have paid for ballet classes and soccer cleats—*thank you.*

To the Gramps who FaceTime whenever our children want them to, you always make yourself available—*thank you.*

To the Grannies who sing the best songs and know just how to calm our little ones down—*thank you.*

To the Nonnas who teach our children how to make Italian lemon cookies—*thank you.* (And for including them in the baking process. They get so excited!)

To be honest, I feel I can never repay my parents and in-laws for all they do for us. I wish I could win the lottery and treat them to an elaborate, all-expense-paid trip to wherever they want. I wish I could buy them new cars, send them to the spa, or wipe some of their worries away.

For now, I will shout from the rooftops how much I love them.

I appreciate you. I am so grateful for you. I need you. I applaud you. I thank you. I couldn't do this without you.

You are so very loved.

Thank You for Being Our Best Friend

JUSTINE LORELLE LOMONACO

When I handed my midwife my birth plan, complete with the list of people I wanted in the room when my daughter was born, she raised an eyebrow. "That's . . . a lot of people," she said. I smiled. "I know, but they're my team." She shrugged, said it shouldn't be a problem, and continued with my exam.

From the first moment I knew I was pregnant, there was no doubt in my mind that you, my best friend, would be a part of it. You are the village I had heard about but never expected to find. You are the shoulder I cry on, the ear that listens patiently to my (endless) baby anecdotes, the arms that hold me when my own feel ready to give out.

When I think back to my daughter's first year of life, there were *so* many moments when I felt alone.

But for every isolating moment of new motherhood, you were there waiting in the wings to prop me up—again—to answer my first-thing-in-the-morning texts, reassuring me that everything was normal, to let me know I was doing a good job. You were there on my doorstep with food (and a bottle of wine) because "It seemed like you were having a hard day."

Your love was like a soft spot to land on at a time when I felt surrounded by rough edges and steep learning curves. I will always be indebted to you for that. But even more, I am incredibly grateful for the love you showed my child.

As much as you held me during that first year, you held my baby just as close.

Thank you for being there from the beginning—from her first breath. You were in the room the moment I met my daughter, helping me labor, catching every moment on video so I could truly be present.

Thank you for holding my baby when I couldn't anymore. I was caught off guard by how physically tiring motherhood was. And when I was at my most exhausted, suddenly you would swoop in like the fairy godmother you are, eager to hold her while I could finally rest.

Thank you for seeing me through my baby's stormy days. I worried you would judge me when I couldn't calm my daughter, but you didn't. You rocked and soothed my fussy baby as long as she needed. You have always seen the best in her, and I will always be grateful for that.

Thank you for making me believe that I can do this. From listening to me cry during my baby's first few nights of sleep training or after a particularly difficult tantrum to cheering us on when we first tried solid foods or ventured into potty training, you were there.

Above all, in the moments I doubted myself the most, you were there, reminding me that I *could do this*.

I catch so many magical moments between you and my child. The whispered secrets while you keep her busy so I can finish shopping. The way she sleepily twirls your hair in the back seat of the car while we run errands around town. The belly laughs you share while you teach her to bake a cake or read her a favorite book.

I hope you know how special you are to us both. While we *might* be able to do this life without you, we're both glad we don't have to even consider that possibility. You have both of our hearts, and you take the best care of them. Thank you for loving my child as much as you love me. Thank you for being our best friend.

They Just Get It

EMILY GLOVER

As I dreamed of what motherhood would be like, fellow mamas were always part of the vision. They were right there with me—understanding my woes about sleepless nights, sharing the playground bench while our kids ran around, and willing to meet up for a moms' night out when we needed a break.

I thought it would be easy to make these friends. We'd hit it off at the playground or fall into step while pushing strollers and—*voila!* BFFs. Then I had my first baby, months after moving to a town where I didn't know another soul. To my surprise, my sleepy little newborn wasn't quite the wingman I expected him to be.

While motherhood had transformed me in innumerable ways, I was still the cautious, tentative-to-make-the-first-move person I always was—just now with sleep deprivation and day-four dry shampoo working against me.

I searched for something to do consistently, hoping to making a meaningful connection. I signed up for a mommy-and-me workout class and told myself to give it a few weeks. The first day felt exactly like going to a new school. *Am I wearing the right thing? Will they like me? Will I make any friends?*

My nerves were immediately calmed by the kind, welcoming women who didn't bat an eye when my baby cried during class. As much as I hit it off with several of them, they weren't really my friends.

No, *my friends* revealed themselves in the coming weeks—first, when we sat around after class feeding babies and then when we started to make plans to get together outside of class. We graduated from workout buddies to true friends through a slow-build series of moments—like laughing together over peanut butter smears on yoga pants, listening without judgment about body insecurities, or commiserating over sleep issues.

One of the reasons we connected is because I allowed myself to be vulnerable.

When we ask
How are you doing?
we mean it.

I decided to give myself a break when it came to appearing perfect to these other women. Without this mindset, I never would have left the house. I wanted to be authentic and hoped that, in return, I would attract authentic friendships.

Luckily, they had the same outlook. They shared the real day-to-day moments, not just the Instagram versions of their lives. Each time we talked, we gave ourselves permission to feel pride, not shame. Recognizing that my friends had the same struggles made it much easier to offer myself grace.

In the years since that first meeting, the workout group disbanded, some mamas moved away, and new babies came along. Through it all, we've continued to let each other in, especially during the moments when we felt we were drowning. We knew we needed each other to stay afloat.

We laugh about it now when we make lofty plans to do something productive while the kids play, only to spend the morning drinking coffee and taking turns holding whichever newborn is crying. We don't pass any judgment when we call each other up for a last-minute playdate just because we need some adult conversation.

When we ask *How are you doing?* we mean it.

We cheer, celebrate, and love each other's children. We don't attempt to hide the challenges we experience through the ins and outs of navigating mom life. All of these moments remind us we're in it together.

Among the many things I feared in motherhood, I was scared when I first became a mom that I'd never make friends I could connect with. But, as with many other challenges in motherhood, I eventually learned to trust myself and the process—and so far, so good.

I've met some really supportive women along the way—ones I couldn't picture my life without—and am so grateful to have them in my village. I will make new friends, I'm sure. But I'll *never* forget my first few mom friends who helped make new motherhood a lot less lonely and a lot more fun.

My Virtual Village Is Real

JULI WILLIAMS

When I became a stay-at-home mom with my first child, I was surprised by how lonely I was. My best friend's daughter and mine were a month apart, and although I had envisioned us hanging out all the time, I actually hardly saw them.

I also found it extremely difficult to keep in touch with friends who didn't have kids. It wasn't that we no longer wanted to spend time together; rather, I was dealing with a colicky baby 24/7.

I often remember thinking when my husband came home from work, *Finally! I can have an adult conversation!* I loved how he became my best friend during this time, yet I deeply craved female friendships.

Simply put, I missed my friends.

I tried to attend mommy-and-me groups, meet-ups, and often visited the park so I could meet other moms organically. But I never clicked with the moms I met. They all seemed to already have their village of friends, and I found it hard to create meaningful connections with them. I'm naturally very shy, so meeting new people was a scary part of new motherhood for me. It seemed necessary and natural to *want* to, but I had trouble navigating it. It was intimidating.

One night when my husband was running late getting home from work and my daughter was asleep, I posted a message on social media sharing how lonely motherhood felt for me at times. Suddenly, I was flooded with messages from other moms sharing their similar feelings. I even got a text message from my best friend saying she felt lonely too.

I messaged back and forth with a few moms, and we started to plan the occasional playdate whenever possible. I also made mom friends from far away who I continue to keep in touch with as our kids grow.

Connecting with other moms through social media and texting was something I desperately needed.

I had been trying *so hard* to find my village that I completely missed the fact that they had been around me all along. Just in a new way.

I realized quickly that, as a mom, it can be difficult to get together with friends. Our children get sick, we have new responsibilities that beg for our attention, we have different nap and sleep schedules, and we have different children who need different things from us—all making in-person get-togethers a bit challenging to plan.

That's why my heart swells with gratitude for my virtual village.

These are my close-knit mama friends who I share so much with, like getting through a tantrum and sleep deprivation or sharing about my daughter's first words or our recent date nights. It feels natural to have them alongside me on this journey.

Yes, motherhood in this day and age looks much different from how our moms created their villages. What I'm learning is that everyone's village looks different. A bulk of mine is online. As part of yours, you may have your mom and sisters or your best friend and brother. Friends from your place of worship or your neighbors may also make up your community. It varies from person to person. And honestly, it doesn't matter what yours looks like—what matters is that you have a strong one to lean on.

Our Caregivers Are Love Givers

JACQUELINE MUNRO TAPP

The first time my partner and I hired a nanny, we were rookie parents. I was a nervous wreck returning to work after an insular twelve-week maternity leave. Becoming a mother had made me doubt if I'd *ever* want to go back to work. Previous dedication and passion for my career aside, the intensity of this newfound love and responsibility of motherhood made me question the idea of leaving my son in someone else's care.

Nevertheless, I returned to work. I felt I owed it to myself to try to reconnect with that pre-mom part of me.

I tentatively reentered the workforce in a role that felt oddly the same, which was surprising because I felt wholly different.

The first day away from my son—in a socially acceptable outfit, including both pants *and* shoes—felt long. It was as though I'd entered a different realm of existence. I awkwardly stumbled through it, scheduling pumping sessions around meetings, bolstered by the photos our nanny sent me, like the one of my son in the stroller peacefully napping while out for a walk.

Each photo I received helped me feel a little stronger. A little more reassured to see how happy and safe he was, without me.

I ran home from the train that evening, smiling like a goon at the prospect of holding my baby again. After our reunion, I hugged our nanny just as hard. She had made my return to work possible. We had all made it through day one.

In the days and weeks that followed, I toughened up a bit. I settled into a schedule of kissing my son goodbye early in the morning, pumping throughout my workday, and commuting home with a cooler-o'-milk each night.

I'd be lying if I claimed it was ever truly easy to leave him with someone else, but I took solace in that he was learning to exist without me. And let's be serious—I was learning to exist without him too.

My son now attends a nursery school, where we quickly grew appreciative of the hard work, love, and support his teachers provide. In fact, as parents of just one toddler who at times pushes us beyond our limits, my husband and I stand in *awe* of their limitless patience in a sea of toddlers.

So, to the nannies, teachers, and childcare providers who are helping to raise our children, I want to say: Thank you!

Thank you for allowing us to stay connected with the other parts of ourselves—to work and provide for our families . . . for being our arms when we aren't present to hold our children, comforting them when they are sad and rocking them to sleep . . . for being our eyes and ears when we are away.

Thank you for sharing the photos, videos, and stories of what our children said, did, and learned in our absence (these help us deal with our parenting FOMO in a big way) . . . for watching our children while we enjoy the occasional (and much-needed!) date night or time reconnecting with friends . . . for giving us peace of mind—when our children are in your care, we are able to relax, knowing they are with you.

We couldn't do this without you.

And now I know that nannies and au pairs and day-care providers don't take something from us; instead, they give us the gift of a loving village for our children.

When There Is No Village

BETH BERRY

Dear mothers,

I'm writing you today because I can no longer contain the ache in my gut and fire in my heart over an injustice that you and I are bearing the brunt of.

The injustice is this: It takes a village, but rarely does a mother have the support of an actual village.

By village I don't simply mean "a group of houses and associated buildings, larger than a hamlet and smaller than a town, situated in a rural area." I'm referring to the way of life inherent to relatively small, relatively contained, multigenerational communities. Communities within which individuals know one another well; share the joys, burdens, and sorrows of everyday life; nurture one another in times of need; mind the well-being of each other's ever-roaming children and increasingly dependent elderly; and feel fed by their clearly essential contribution to the group that securely holds them.

I'm talking about the most natural environment for children to grow up in.

I'm talking about a way of life we are biologically wired for but is nearly impossible to find in developed nations.

I'm talking about the primary unmet need driving the frustration that most every villageless mother is feeling.

Although we may say it "takes a village to raise a child," virtually none of us have that village, and it's wreaking havoc on our quality of life in countless ways.

In the absence of the village, enormous pressure is put on parents as we try to make up for what entire communities used to provide. We feel less safe and more anxious without the known boundaries, expectations, and support of a well-known group of people with whom to grow. And we are forced to create our villages during seasons of our life when we have the least time and energy to do so. We run around wild, trying to make up for the interaction, stimulation, and learning opportunities that were once within walking distance.

Our priorities become distorted and unclear as we attempt to meet so many conflicting needs at once.

We forget what "normal" looks and feels like, which leaves us feeling as if we're not doing enough—or enough of the "right" things. We spend money we don't have on things we don't need in an attempt to fill the voids we feel. And we rely heavily on social media for a sense of connection, which works for some but leads others of us to feel even more isolated and inadequate.

Without a village we may feel guilty for just about everything: not wanting or having time to be our children's primary playmates, not working enough, working too much, allowing too much screen time in order to keep up with our million perceived responsibilities, and so on. Joy, lightness, and fun feel hard to access. We think we're supposed to be independent and feel ashamed of our need for others.

We may even make decisions that reflect our deeply unmet needs instead of our values.

Perhaps most tragically of all, the absence of the village is distorting many mothers' sense of self. It's causing us to feel that our inadequacies are to blame for our struggles, which further perpetuates the feeling that we must do even *more* to make up for them.

Here's a new mindset to try on for size.

You and I are not the problem. We are doing plenty. We may feel inadequate, but that's because we're on the front lines of the problem—we're the ones being hardest hit. We absorb the impact of a broken, still-oppressive social structure so that our children won't have to. But that makes us *heroes*, not failures.

I've tasted village life before. My soul was fed deeply during those times. Every time I get a taste of what we're missing, I become strengthened and hopeful again. And while I have no idea what the future holds, I do know this: We're supposed to be crying, celebrating, falling down, and rising together. We're supposed to have grandmothers and aunts and neighbors and cousins and friends sharing the everyday moments, guiding us and helping us see the sacredness in the chaotic.

We're supposed to be nurtured for months postpartum, cared for when we're sick, held while we mourn, and supported during challenging transitions.

So, here's what I think we should do.

I think we should lead with vulnerability and let our people know when things aren't going okay in our lives. We should believe them when they say they want to help, and actually accept their help when they offer it. Then, when it's our turn, we can extend the same gift of love and support to a kindred mama ourselves. We should open our hearts and build our community—and truly be in this together.

Here with you,
A fellow mama

practice
BUILDING YOUR VILLAGE

BETH BERRY

You and I aren't likely to experience what it's like to raise children in an *actual* village, like many mothers who have come before us. But that's okay. That's not what this generation is about. *This* generation is about waking up to who we really are and what we really want, and resetting society's sails accordingly.

Playing your part in the re-villaging of our culture starts with being wholly, unapologetically, courageously *you*.

Here are a few tangible steps you can take whenever you're ready:

1. **Get really clear on one thing: You need and deserve help.** The fact that you're struggling is not a reflection of your inadequacies but the unnatural cultural circumstances you're living within.

2. **Own and honor your needs.** Most mothers are walking around with several deeply unmet needs of their own while focusing almost exclusively on the needs of others. This is precisely the thing that keeps us from gaining traction and improving our circumstances, both individually and collectively.

3. **Practice vulnerability.** Rich, safe, authentic connection is essential for thriving. Cultivating this quality of connection takes courage and a willingness to step outside your comfort zone. What you want most exists on the other side of that initial awkward conversation or embarrassing introduction.

4. **Own your strengths.** What makes you feel strong and fully alive? What lights you up and gives you energy just thinking about it?

Who would be in your village if you had one? Tapping into your strengths and engaging them is one of the greatest ways to attract the kinds of people you want in your life, bless and inspire others, and build a sense of community in ways that fill rather than drain you.

5. **Become an integral part of something.** Whether it's a knitting group, dance troupe, church, kayaking club, or homeschool collective, commit to growing a community around one area of your life that enlivens you or fills a need. Use the connections you cultivate within this community to practice showing up bravely and authentically and asking for what you need, whether that's support, resources, or encouragement.

6. **Do your part and ONLY *your* part.** Though it's tempting to fill our lives to the brim with commitments that make a difference, doing so only further disempowers us. Read *Essentialism* by Greg McKeown if you struggle with this one.

7. **Learn self-love and self-compassion.** In a culture of "never enough," it is essential that we forge healthy relationships with ourselves to be able to fend off the many messages hitting us about who we're meant to be and what makes us worthy of happiness and love. In fact, I see self-love in action as the greatest gift our generation of mothers could possibly give to the mothers of tomorrow.

8. **Speak your truth.** Be true to yourself and the path you're on by standing up for yourself. Even when you're terrified. Even if it makes you the bravest one in the room.

9. **Imagine a new way.** Where we're headed looks nothing like where we've come from. Creating the kind of future we want requires envisioning that future and believing a new way to be possible. Get specific and think big. What do *you* want?

journal QUESTIONS

- Who are your lifelines, those who support you and your family's well-being, and those who simply add goodness to your life? For the next five days, take two minutes each evening to reflect on and write about this. You may notice a pattern.

- How might you express gratitude or appreciation for the people in your village? Consider something as simple as a short note or a heartfelt thank-you next time you see each other.

Transformation

I didn't lose myself when I became a mother. I found myself.
ANONYMOUS

INTRODUCTION

LIZ TENETY

Motherhood changes everything—your breasts, your body, your brain. And if you're like many women, it changes your job, your home, your car, your relationship, your finances, and your shoe size too—not to mention the time you wake up, go to sleep, and the precious time you spend alone in the bathroom—it's all different. But here's the powerful secret: So much of motherhood changes you for the *better*.

We become more compassionate to others going through struggle. We find new focus and efficiency at work, pushing through deadlines during nap time. We discover deep reserves of energy after many sleepless nights. Beyond the demands and struggles—the relentlessness of it all—we find something surprising: our superpowers.

I became so much more productive at work after I had my baby.

I also was able to get organized—something I'd struggled for years to do—because life demanded I stay on top of my paperwork and schedule. Instead of a life full of unmet dreams and regrets, I rose to the occasion and actually began to live up to my own expectations of myself—because that's what motherhood demanded of me.

I finally was able to become the person I always wanted to be.

As you read this section, consider the ways that motherhood has transformed you and taught you to embrace the amazing woman you've become. While you may mourn the life you've left behind (RIP, brunch), we hope you'll also celebrate the powerful, loving, capable woman who's been molded by motherhood.

P.S. We've included affirmations at the end of this section to encourage you to see the beauty in your superpowers. Read and repeat these phrases whenever you need to remind yourself just how awesome you are. You may not be perfect, but you are the perfect mother for your child.

Metamorphosis of a Mother

DIANA SPALDING

I'm a midwife and was also the first of my friends to become a mom, so I tend to get a lot of questions from people. Once, when my children were four, sixteen months, and one month (just writing that makes me tired), a good friend with a newborn called to ask, "When do you get the hang of all this?" I chuckled and said honestly, "I'm not sure. I'll let you know when it happens."

I still can't wrap my mind around the fact that *I am somebody's mother.*

Three somebodies, in fact. I still feel like a little girl figuring out the world. I vividly remember dreaming about becoming a mom. When I was about twelve, I looked up at Orion's Belt and told my parents that I was going to have three kids—one for each star.

Life with my little stars is spent in a chaotic swirl of love and activity, trying to keep it all together. When I reflect on it, it takes my breath away. I don't think there was one moment when I suddenly *became* a mother—it was more a collection of tiny moments that created me.

I transformed a little more into a mother . . . when I uprooted my entire life to create a safe and desirable home for my future children . . . when I laid eyes on my future husband for the first time and fell instantly in love with him (and hoped our kids would get his smile) . . . when, just two days after my first positive pregnancy test, I thought I was losing the pregnancy and cried harder and more gut-wrenchingly than ever before. (I cried even harder when I found out that I was still pregnant.)

I transformed a little more into a mother . . . when, after a thirty-two-hour labor and my postpartum room was cleared of visitors, it was just me and my brand-new baby daughter in the still of the night. She stirred, and without a moment of hesitation, I was holding her in my arms, a wave of profound power ripping through my chest—*I am a mother. I am her mother.*

I transformed a little more into a mother . . . when I was the only one who correctly diagnosed the reason behind my second child's constant crying. I stood up for him, and for us. I fought for him, and I became his hero.

I transformed a little more into a mother . . . when I breastfed our third child for the last time. The sun shone through the window onto his face, and every time we made eye contact he burst into laughter and unlatched. I wept with sadness and appreciation and awe of it all.

With every milestone, every knowing exchange of glances with another mom, every kissed boo-boo, doctor appointment, laugh, setback, worry, collapse into bed, and deep breath, I become a little more *mother* than I was the moment before.

Truthfully, I don't think I'll ever get the hang of it. How could I? How could any of us possibly get used to the all-consuming love and rawness and vulnerability that motherhood brings?

I don't know that we ever do, really. All I can do is love my children with all my heart—when it aches, when it leaps with joy—and remember that whenever I feel lost, my stars are right there alongside me, lighting my path to help guide me and lighting my life to help sustain me.

This Body Is Beauty

EMILY GLOVER

Most days I don't recognize the person in the mirror. Her belly isn't firm. Her hair isn't styled. Her face is getting deeper creases. Her hips are striped with stretch marks. Her arms aren't defined. Her legs are checkered with cellulite. Her breasts are saggy.

And, for once in my life, I think she's beautiful.

This was the belly that grew two babies . . .

These are the graying hairs that have been pulled and twirled by little hands . . .

These are the lines caused by laughter at toddler antics . . .

This is the skin that stretched while turning two cells into new human beings . . .

These are the soft arms that have cradled newborns . . .

These are the dimpled legs that swayed with sleepy babies in the middle of the night . . .

These are the breasts that sustained little lives for months and months . . .

This is the body that has been given a greater purpose.

Motherhood has given me the gift of finally believing that my body is *worthy*. After all, the evidence is just down the hall, asleep in their bedrooms.

Does this mean I never wish my belly were firmer? No, I would still love those jeans to glide right over my hips as easily as they used to. But I wouldn't trade the mindset I have today for the body I used to have.

I know now that self-love doesn't mean being blind to our ever-changing, ever-aging human bodies. It means appreciating them for those very reasons.

Through the years, my relationship with my body ran the spectrum from reluctant acceptance to active dislike. More energy was poured into molding my legs, abs, or arms into better versions than was spent loving my body just as it was. It was just flaws, gripes, and an impossible quest to reach some number on the scale. I knew that having a goal of perfection would always end in disappointment, but I didn't know what the alternative was.

Then I saw two pink lines on a pregnancy test.

Suddenly, my body wasn't just mine to manipulate and challenge; it was a home for my baby.

This is the body that has been given a greater purpose.

Knowing this allowed me to treat my body with grace. Yes, those concerns were still there, but now they were overtaken by feelings of love and gratitude.

For the next nine months, as the magnitude of what my body was doing sank in, the space in my heart and mind that was once reserved for negative self-talk got smaller and smaller. Each weekly bump photo or heartbeat scan was a reminder of the amazing process: Without doing much of anything intentionally—except prenatal vitamins and regular OB/GYN checkups—I was growing a new human being. My body was transforming.

Then, without me even having to *think* about it, my body knew how to give birth. The power and strength were in me all along, and I couldn't help but feel empowered by it. I also started to reflect on all the ways I had taken my body for granted before.

My body isn't amazing because it's perfect, but because it's enabled me to live a beautiful life.

These days photos of my body would need Photoshopping to fit into a magazine. But my body also brought two new lives into the world, nourished them, and continues to be a safe space for my children when they're in need of a lap or chest to nestle into. I see no greater purpose. And now, finally, I have the clarity to appreciate how beautiful my body *really* is.

When You Have
to Leave for Work

ALICIA KESWANI

Hey there, working mama,

I want you to know that I know how it feels.

I know the guilt you feel as you dry your hair in the morning and the baby watches you from a bouncy seat. I know the sting that pierces your heart when you hand your precious little one to their caretaker and you catch excitement in the baby's eyes—that irrational fear that they will think someone else is their mama or that this person is doing a better job than you.

I know how it feels—and it may be the most painful thought for me personally—to believe your caretaker knows your baby better than you do. I know the fatigue that sets in when all you feel is guilt: guilt when you enjoy going to work and guilt when you want to go home early to be with your baby. There's guilt when you miss a milestone or have to stay late to catch up on a project . . . when you forget about an upcoming meeting or have to leave early because the baby got sick . . . when it's been three months back at work and it *still* doesn't feel normal yet.

I know what it feels like to try to make sense of this complicated transformation to "working mom" when you feel like you only *just* started to begin to understand the transformation to "mom."

I know that sometimes you go cry in a bathroom stall when you are so very overwhelmed. I did the same thing last week. I know the sadness you feel when you overhear your coworkers plan an impromptu happy hour and you can't join them. I know the loneliness that settles into your heart as you learn how to juggle this new life. I know you question if you are good enough—good enough at work, good enough as a mom, and good enough as a partner. I've felt all of these emotions too.

Hear me, friend. We may not know each other, but I do know this: You were chosen to be your baby's mama.

> You were chosen to be your baby's mama.

Right now you are choosing to work—or you *have* to work. But you are not just "mom," and you are not just "employee." All of who you are—your passions, your fears, your job, your living situation, your marital status, your heart, your soul—is being used to create something so precious: a childhood. You are not a bad mama for working. You are not a bad employee because you are a mom.

If you are working a job you hate but you do it because bills don't pay themselves, you are providing the means to create a childhood with a safe place to sleep and good things to eat. And I pray that one day you'll get to do the job you love the most—be it in a different workplace or in your home.

If you are working a job you love, and you do it because you are passionate for your cause, you are providing the example for little girls to grow up and achieve their dreams and for little boys to see their moms, sisters, aunts, and future daughters as equally capable.

Either way, you are working because you are a great mother. So I hope you'll transform the narrative in your own mind: Your working is an act of love. It may take time, but both you and your children will one day see it that way too.

You are not alone in navigating this path, though it can feel very lonely at times. When the days blur together and the routine becomes mind-numbing, I pray that you'll choose to see those days and moments as small pieces of a beautiful picture: the childhood you've been entrusted to create.

You are brave, and I admire you.

Love,
A fellow working mama

The Stay-at-Home Mom I Always Wanted to Be

JESSICA JOHNSTON

I have heard the dreaded question: What *do* stay-at-home moms do all day? I have contemplated my purpose: *Is my life's work supposed to be full of diaper changes and tantrum taming?* I have wondered about my worth: *My children [aka my bosses] haven't given me a four-star yearly review just yet; do they understand how much I do for them? Do they appreciate it?*

Well, to answer the question of what we do all day, I can promise you we are *not* at home having a day off. And I swear I do *a lot* and don't always feel accomplished at the end of the day.

Sometimes the days are so long, and there's no end in sight to the countless tasks we're presented with daily.

We clean things . . . Not to brag, but my kids can turn my house into a major health code violation in ten seconds flat—usually right before someone stops by.

We smell things . . . pillows, clothes, car seats. We're always asking, "Did someone poop?" "Is that food under there?"

We do laundry . . . We are literally *always* doing laundry:

STEP 1	Wash load.
STEP 2	Forget.
STEP 3	Smell load.
STEP 4	Hmm. Smells fine. Dry load.
STEP 5	Smell dry clothes.
STEP 6	Nooooo.
STEP 7	Rewash and dry.
STEP 8	Pull out dry clothes to fold "later" and throw them on your bed.
STEP 9	Forget until you go to bed. UGH.
STEP 10	Throw clothes on floor.
STEP 11	In the morning watch as children run through clothes until you can no longer tell what is clean.
STEP 12	Throw pile back on bed because you cannot even.
STEP 13	Repeat until you die.

We keep people alive . . . We save lives, one pair of adult scissors at a time. We deliver children places . . . I'm just a girl, sitting in a minivan on the way to school, from school, to birthday parties, to dance, to sports.

We feed people . . . I serve up three meals a day so that people can cry, fall on the floor in convulsions, and agonize over which is better: my cooking or starving.

We go grocery shopping . . . In addition to toddlers in tow, we make moral and economic decisions at the grocery store: Do I spend my life savings on organic, or do I fill my cart with hormones and pesticides and feel like a money-saving boss?

We are not searching for unsolicited advice. Things you can do instead of giving me advice? Clean my minivan, pour me a coffee, get me a Roomba that eats toys, or tell me I'm pretty. That's all.

We are not judging you. And we don't have time for judging. I do not care if your kid eats fruit snacks or cucumbers. I don't care if you homeschool or are a working mom.

I don't think my life is harder or that I'm some sort of martyr. I think it's exactly what I chose—and sometimes it's hard because that's the nature of things that matter.

Just like any great dream, it's worth the cost.

So, what do stay-at-home moms do all day? Well, I'd like to think we're creating homes, happiness, and childhoods. I may look tired (and I am!) and I may vent at times, but, ultimately, my transformation over the years to stay-at-home mom has given me the life I've always wanted.

When You Want It All

COLLEEN TEMPLE

I love being a mother. It's a vocation that always called to me and one I happily fulfilled—from taking a birthing class and documenting my growing bump to navigating breastfeeding and figuring out my baby's different cries. I loved this new part of my identity.

I threw myself into the role of "mom." And I found a lot of joy in those first few months of motherhood, both in the great moments and the not-so-great moments, because I learned a lot about who I am and what I'm made of.

One of the things I learned was that I missed identifying as a working professional. I loved motherhood, but I often found myself longing for something in addition to my new #momlife.

I had always worked, and I missed the validation of coming up with good ideas or the satisfaction of having a creative outlet. I missed contributing to my family financially. So I got a job.

Even though there is passion and purpose in the job I have—and even though I feel like my career is very much a part of who I am—sometimes I feel guilty that I'm not dedicating *all* my time to my kids. Sometimes I desperately miss focusing solely on being "mom." Some days I wish I stayed home with them. They are so small, growing and developing so fast. Am I missing important moments? Probably. Could we do without the money I bring in? Doubtful. Some days my heart aches with these worries.

Therefore, I've decided I want to be a stay-at-home mom *and* a working mom. I want to be defined by many different factors in my life — work and children included.

I know I want to be the one who is always

- around to take care of my kids: to cook for them, put them down for their naps, get them dressed

- there to comfort them: to hold them when they cry, kiss their boo-boos, rock them to sleep

- ready to take them on adventures: to the park, the farm, the library

- there to do the mundane things: to pick them up at school, remind them to brush their teeth, help them find their shoes

- available to play with them: to read them exciting books, act out scenes from *Moana*, show them how to throw a ball

- there to teach them important life lessons: to show them how to be kind and remind them to protect each other

But I also want to be on a team with other adults working toward a common goal.

I want to be part of the creative process, solve a problem, give my opinion, speak up when I have an idea, learn from intelligent minds, grow as a professional, and challenge my brain by developing a new skill.

I guess I want the best of both worlds. Is this possible? Yes *and* no.

I am now a thirty-hour-a-week work-from-home mom with a part-time nanny who watches my children at our house. I work at Motherly, where I am valued for my role of "editor" and respected for my role of "mother"; where it's understood that my role of "parent" comes first; where some days, I breastfeed my baby while I'm on a virtual team call or I am interrupted on said team call because my two-year-old decided to bust into my office to read me a story; where I take a break for lunch *and* to drop my four-year-old off at preschool; where I can multitask by writing an essay on my phone while I put my eight-month-old down for her nap.

I now realize that the balance of work life and home life will always need recalibrating. It's never going to be perfect, and it's not always going to stay the same. What it comes down to is: Whether I work or not, I am a good mom, and my children are well taken care of (by me and other people as well). They feel safe and loved. That's what's important.

> But I also want to be on a team with other adults working toward a common goal.

My number-one priority is to show my children that I would do anything for them—and sometimes that includes following my dreams outside of motherhood.

These dreams are so much a part of who I am. They have helped me feel like a better, stronger version of myself for my family. And so, as I evolve over time into the many different versions of "me" that I'll be, I'll remember that motherhood is not defined by how many deadlines I had in a day or how many boo-boos I patched up in a week—just like how I'm not defined solely by whether I work or not.

I am redefining what it means for me to be a working mom, boo-boo by boo-boo, deadline by deadline, day by day.

My Sons Transformed My View of Men

LIZ TENETY

I don't buy into gender stereotypes much. I know my two sons have male parts and testosterone coursing through their veins, but I try not to read too much into their sex. One of my boys loves quietly reading books and coloring pictures. The other loves screaming, running, and punching things. Born eighteen months apart, they're both mine and completely unique individuals. I consider them both "all boy."

Having sons has helped me connect with men in a whole new way.

Becoming a parent truly transforms how you see the world. Growing up as a girl, I always saw boys as "the other." The feminist in me read stories about male privilege and the glass ceiling and saw men as part of the problem—keeping women out of power and even sacred spaces. I knew men, but I never *identified with* boys until I became a boy mom.

I first realized how motherhood changed me when watching a news story about a police officer who had been shot and killed while on duty. In the past, I would have watched the report, which included an interview with his mother, and thought *Oh, how sad* and swiftly moved on.

But that night—with my nine-month-old firstborn son sleeping in the bedroom next door—a deep, gut-level response washed over me. Tears filled my eyes. A lump swelled in my throat. *That poor man. That poor mother.* That police officer was her baby.

I was equally surprised to discover the sweet affection I suddenly felt toward young teenage boys. I've watched these unsure boys—full of acne and hormones, awkwardness and aspiration—walk down the sidewalk in our town and felt a powerful maternal instinct. In only a handful of years, my baby will be one of these creatures: a sweaty, crush-obsessed, boy-turning-into-a-man. I can't help but look at these fourteen-year-olds and smile.

Those teenage boys are other moms' babies.

I saw an old man in the coffee shop last week. His hands shook as he fumbled to bring his coffee cup to his lips. He kept to himself, maintaining his independence as well as he could muster with his cane. His mother is most likely not here anymore. But he did have a mother. And I'd like to think that she loved him fiercely until the end of her days. That old man was somebody's baby.

My husband is a wonderful man and father. Becoming a parent taught me that good men don't just show up fully formed. They are molded, pushed, and nurtured in thousands of small and large ways. And I am so grateful for the good man his mama raised. He's a wonderful husband now, but he'll always be his mother's baby.

Someday my boys won't have their sweet little voices and soft little bodies. They'll be large and limby, too busy for me. Thinking of their angel faces with facial hair makes me laugh—and cry. My boys will always be my babies.

> Having sons has helped me connect with men in a whole new way.

But my little boys will someday become men. Big men with big responsibilities and burdens weighing them down. With cultural notions of masculinity to accept or reject. With the opportunity to be tender or heroic—or both. With their own conceptions of what it means to be a "good man."

It's an honor to help guide, raise, and launch my little men.

No matter how big my sons get, they'll always fit perfectly inside my heart.

I will always feel a warmth and depth of connection with men around the world because of these darling boys of mine.

And they will *always* be my babies.

My Daughters Made Me Confident

COLLEEN TEMPLE

I was painfully shy growing up. I panicked when randomly called on in class and would do anything to avoid having to speak up in general. I followed my older sister around like her shadow so I wouldn't have to socialize on my own.

This continued through high school, into college, and followed me to my first few jobs after graduating. I would turn bright red when I had to speak in meetings and would second-guess bringing an idea to my boss. I could barely talk on the phone in my cubicle because people would hear me speak.

Then I became a mother. And instead of just having my coworkers' eyes on me, my three daughters are now watching my every move.

Motherhood hasn't cured my shyness completely, but it *has* encouraged me to open up in ways I never would have before children.

Why? Because it has pushed me (way) out of my comfort zone, because I want to model confidence and self-assuredness for my daughters, and because motherhood makes you rise to the occasion no matter what.

I love this new freedom. I have a strong sense of what I'm good at, what I like, and what areas I could use some work in. So now it's time for me to really own every piece of that, to be gentle with myself, to forgive myself when I make mistakes, and to push myself to be better.

Part of that clear sense of self is to continue to show my girls what an empowered woman looks and acts like—what she does, and who she is.

I always knew in my heart that I'd have daughters. And I decided when my first daughter was born four years ago that it would be my mission to raise young women who believe in themselves and all of their vast abilities; women who believe in their power and understand that they can do anything they set out to do; women who believe that they deserve to be heard, that their opinions are valid, that they *should* take up space, and that their minds are beautiful.

I encourage my daughters to use their words and to look people in the eye when they have something to say. I explain that sometimes people aren't going to want to hear what they have to say, but if it means a lot to them, it's important to say it anyway.

Being brave often means doing things that are scary.

I model positive self-talk and I don't speak negatively about myself—my body included—in front of my girls. I have flaws and I'm not always happy with my reflection in the mirror, but I don't let them in on these thoughts and feelings. I show them how to treat themselves with grace and patience. When I have regrets about the way I said or did something, I acknowledge it so that they feel safe making mistakes too.

> Being brave
> often means
> doing things
> that are scary.

We often say these words together—"I'm brave, I'm powerful, I'm strong, I'm confident, I'm intelligent, I'm kind, I'm funny, and I'm silly"—because I want them to believe them.

I want them to raise their hand in class. To use their voice to speak out on issues they believe in. To know it's okay to say no. I want them to confidently explain concepts they grasp and ideas they have. I want them to not be afraid to ask questions, to tell jokes without the fear of looking "dumb," and to start conversations with someone who is sitting alone.

My children have given me the incredible gift of confidence. And I want to share this gift with them every day.

Stepping Into Stepmom

RACHEL GORTON

They say nothing can prepare you for motherhood, and "they" are right. Seven years ago I became a mom, and just like *that* . . . my world changed. Despite the advice, books, and guidance, I felt unprepared for the journey ahead of me. But after seven years, I feel like I have gotten the hang of the mom thing.

However, I'm still trying to figure out my new-*ish* role as a stepmom. There's a lot of information to guide you as you prepare for motherhood, but stepparenting requires a completely separate manual. It comes with its own set of challenges, hardships, and celebratory moments, which are pretty confusing to navigate.

When I married my husband, I knew I was also "marrying" his three kids and that it would be an adjustment. What I didn't realize was that becoming a stepmom would transform me into a whole new kind of woman and mother.

Stepkids don't "have" to love you back. And navigating the hurt of separation, divorce, or death can be incredibly tricky for them.

But by wanting the best for these children who aren't my own by birth—and loving them without expectations—I've learned that motherhood exists beyond the borders I'd imagined.

We might not share DNA, yet my role as a mother is no less significant to those I love and care about. Those I *mother*.

I mother my stepchildren each time I worry for them and their well-being.

I mother my stepchildren when I have to make decisions that might not make me very popular but I know will be better for them in the long run.

I mother my stepchildren when I believe in them and push them to do better. I mother them and I mother those who aren't even my children.

I mother friends at church when they are sick or in need.

I mother a stranger who I can see is struggling and needs some encouragement.

I mother my sisters when they need guidance and direction.

I mother myself when I stop judging and holding myself to a standard I would never hold anyone else to.

Becoming a stepmother has taught me that motherhood is about *much* more than biology. It is about selflessly pouring myself into the relationships in my life and the world around me.

It is about praying for others and genuinely wanting the best for them.

It is about loving without conditions and being willing to put my heart on the line a million times.

It is about enduring emotional exhaustion and daily crises with grace and forgiveness.

It is about wanting my children and my stepchildren to be the best they can be. To feel loved and accepted and important.

As a stepmother, I have been pushed to limits I didn't know were possible. In the process, I have developed a deeper understanding of my abilities as a woman, wife, and mother.

And along the way, I have evolved into a more compassionate human.

Now and Then

LIZ TENETY

Do you ever catch sight of a woman who looks like you—before you had kids?

Early weekday mornings she's rushing to work. She's checking email, browsing Instagram. She's got a lot on her plate and a lot to do, but she's also got time for things like spin class and carefree outings with friends.

On the weekends she sleeps in until 10:00 a.m. and then lounges at brunch with her friends—seemingly without a care in the world. Her outfit is on trend. She's recently showered. She has worries and fears and stressors, of course—but they're not as outwardly visible to a watchful eye. She might have kids one day, but her mind cannot fathom what becoming a mother will do to her life. She just doesn't know.

That woman was me.

Now, mornings look like this: Push SNOOZE—again—when my 5:00 a.m. alarm goes off. Wake up an hour later to the sound of "MOOOOOOOOM!" Check work emails and take deep breaths to deal with the anxiety of completing the day's tasks. Gulp down as much coffee as humanly possible. Frantically brush teeth, apply dry shampoo (again), and put on semiclean pants over my baby bump. (No, I'm not pregnant, but I do still have that bump.)

Quickly pack lunches, convince several small humans to put their coats on, and make our way to school and work before we're late.

Still me. Still the morning. But it's a whole new life.

I sometimes fantasize about my life before kids, and long for all the things I deeply miss. I think about what I could have had if I'd chosen not to add a bunch of tiny humans to the mix. And honestly, sometimes I long for that life.

I could have had quiet mornings to sip my coffee and listen to my favorite podcasts in peace. Instead of quiet mornings, I have the voices of three little people chirping for breakfast.

I could have had weekends to sleep in. Instead, I have family bonding time.

> Still me.
> Still the morning.
> But it's a
> whole new life.

I could have had *way* more money in the bank. Instead, I have a mortgage and a safe place for my kids to sleep and a wonderful au pair who loves our family.

I could have had a cool car. Instead, I have a functional one that gets us to preschool and back, safely.

I could have traveled around the world. London, Paris, Jerusalem, and Beijing remain on my bucket list. Instead, I have cheap vacations crashing with family and friends.

I could have had sexy, monthly getaways with my husband. Instead of endless alone time with my husband, I have an incredible father for our children.

I could have had perfectly styled hair and a killer wardrobe. Instead of a daily shower, I have a dry shampoo and a mom-bun.

I could have had a beautifully designed home full of the perfect furniture. Instead, I have a playroom full of art supplies and a kitchen floor dotted with Cheerios.

I could have had a perfectly smooth belly, without stretch marks or stretched skin or childbearing hips. Instead, I have acceptance of my body—and grace for myself when acceptance is hard.

I could have belonged to the cool gym with the chill instructors. Instead, I go to the affordable one with free childcare.

I could have been free to do whatever I wanted, whenever I wanted.

I could have had that life. And sometimes I dream of it.

But instead of all of that, I have these three little gifts that I wouldn't trade for all the money, flat stomachs, and lazy weekends in the world.

My life was validating before—as a single woman with no kids yet, and a blossoming career. My life is validating now as a mother to three children and the cofounder of Motherly.

Perhaps your life is validating . . . in choosing to have an only child . . . or in struggling to conceive and making peace with the unknown of your journey . . . or in deciding that motherhood isn't the right direction right now.

The beauty of life is deciding where each of our paths will take us—for ourselves.

I could have had *me*; instead, I get to have *us*.

practice
AFFIRMATIONS FOR MAMAS

ALLIE CASAZZA

Mama, you are incredible. You have SO much power—power to raise a new generation and change the world. How huge is that?!

What we need to do, from one mother to another, is to *own* that power. We need to own it so well and so completely that nothing anybody says in judgment of our decisions—no matter how condescending the look or snide the remark—can ever stop us from being the force of nature we are. We are strong and beautiful. We are capable and brave. We are doing it—every single day. We hope you feel that for yourself.

If you can't right now, that's okay. We've all been there. But just because you can't feel something doesn't mean it isn't true.

Let these affirmations for mamas help bring this power out in you as you walk the road of motherhood laid out before you. We are all in this together.

Use these affirmations in your daily life by writing them down and placing them somewhere you'll see them (perhaps on your bathroom mirror or on the inside of your front door) at least once a day. Lean on them when you could really use a pick-me-up by taking ten minutes for yourself in a favorite secret quiet spot. Say these affirmations out loud, or in your heart, and let them empower you and bring you a sense of comfort.

- I am enough.

- I am doing my best.

- I am grateful.

- My body is strong; I am proud of all that it has given me.

- I am proud of what I accomplish.

- I am a good mother.

- I see myself with love.

- I do all the important things that my family needs.

- I have all I need.

- I find calm in the storm.

- I am perfect as I am.

- I am supported.

- I am kind.

- I am bold.

- I am powerful.

- I am surrounded by love.

- I am able to see the joy in my life.

- I am the best mother for my child.

journal QUESTIONS

- In what ways have you changed since becoming a mother? How have you changed the most?

- How are you responding to the changes that motherhood brings to your life?

- What are *your* superpowers?

In the Depths

> Being a mother is learning about strengths you didn't know
> you had and dealing with fears you never knew existed.
> **LINDA WOOTEN**

INTRODUCTION

JILL KOZIOL

Women are *so* strong. First there's our physical strength, which allows us to carry a baby, give birth, and take care of our little ones. The toll it takes on our bodies is no joke. We also need to be strong mentally *and* emotionally—especially when we're in the depths of motherhood.

We can be extremely hard on ourselves. When we mess up, we beat ourselves up. We want to *be* all the things for all the people. To *do* all the things for all the people. Too often we forget about our own needs.

Even when our cups are empty, we keep pouring.

There's power in the lows, though, in those deepest depths. That's why I believe in acknowledging and embracing the obstacles we overcome. I'm open about the miscarriage I experienced and the dark days that followed my loss. Everything had been perfect with my first pregnancy, and I took it for granted that everything would be okay with my next. I was wholly unprepared for what happened.

The day I found out I was expecting twins was also the day I found out something was wrong. We spent nearly a month confirming the pregnancy was lost, that both babies were gone, and then waited for my body to let go.

Even with my young daughter, Clare, as a light in my life, I was shattered. I was in denial, I bargained with God, I blamed myself, I couldn't get out of bed. I mourned in a profound way I'd never experienced before.

Kindness and love from my village put me back together. I learned a lot about self-compassion during this low time. I needed to give myself permission to mourn; I needed to be gentle with my heart.

I'm a stronger mama today for the loss I experienced and a more empathetic mom to Clare and my rainbow baby, Cate. I try to model empathy for my daughters by giving it to myself, being honest with them, and asking for forgiveness in a way that's age appropriate.

Last week was stressful, and I snapped at Clare. When I saw the crushed look on her face, I took a deep breath, got to her level, and said, "I'm sorry, Clare. Mommy had a hard week, and it's not your fault I lost my patience. I'll do better next time. Can you forgive me?"

I vividly remember the first time I did this. I was comforting Clare when she was four and shared how I wasn't proud of the way I handled myself.

I admitted I was still learning how to be a mommy and that I was going to make mistakes sometimes.

What happened next was really profound. I could see that Clare *got* it, and in that moment of admitting to my feelings of failure, I realized that I *was* still learning how to be a mommy, and I would actually always be learning—for the rest of my life. That was freeing for me. It helped me let go of my perfectionist tendencies and, rather than beating myself up, move on quicker after a #momfail.

Motherhood is complex and often requires strength we didn't know we had inside, especially in those darkest moments. But you've got this, mama. You were made for it.

P.S. At the end of this section, we've included a writing exercise to help you craft a letter to yourself to extend forgiveness for either a mistake you've made or for any perceived shortcomings you think you have. We hope it helps you let go of the guilt you may be carrying and enables you to have more compassion and grace for yourself.

Mama Said There'd Be Days Like This

COLLEEN TEMPLE

Mama said there'd be days like this. She said there'd be days that would push you to your limits.

Days when you feel so low that you doubt every decision you make.

Days that are bad and scary and test your every nerve.

Days that are so all over the place, you know you're going to forget something.

Days when you wonder if you're doing anything right at all.

Days when you can feel the exhaustion deep in your bones, the worry deep in your heart, the mental load heavy on your mind.

Mama said there'd be days like this. She said there'd be days when you'd feel like you're failing.

Days when you feel like nothing is going right.

Days when you know you let someone down.

Days when you don't leave the house because you can't get it together.

Days when you question why you can't figure this out, why you don't have the answer, and wonder what is wrong with you.

Mama said there'd be days like this. She said there'd be days when you'd question yourself.

Am I doing enough?
Am I present enough?
Am I happy enough?
Am I patient enough?
Did I play enough today?
Plan enough?
Laugh enough?
Am I enough?
We all have these days, I can assure you of that.

And Mama said we'd have the bad days. The dark days. The days when you honestly just don't think you can do this anymore. When those days happen, know this: Mama said there would be days like this. Because there will also be days like this:

The day when your baby says "Mama" for the first time.

The day your toddler discovers how to jump—and can't stop jumping.

The day your preschooler tells you you're "THE BEST MOM IN THE WORLD!" and when she says it, you actually believe her.

The day when your kid starts kindergarten, and she loves it.

The day your kids sleep in and you sleep in and you wake up *finally* feeling refreshed. (It has been known to occasionally happen.)

The day you spend at the park with a packed lunch picnic, and your little family and you realize there is nothing you need more in the world.

The day you feel at peace for the first time in a long time and know you're doing more than all right as a mother. You're doing amazing.

Mama said there'd be days like this. Even on the dark days, trust Mama.

Mama Is Human Too

BRIANNA MOBILIAN

Before I became a mother, I dreamed of the type of mom I would be. It was a magical dream with perfect children and where being a mom was so easy. My strength was the ability to keep my composure through any event. I didn't have to use my patience often, but if I did, it didn't matter because I had an infinite source of it.

Then, when I actually became a mother, it felt easy and natural. It was just like the dream I had. Motherhood felt like a breeze.

So you can imagine my surprise when the first few years passed, and my son proved to be just as human as any other child.

Somewhere between the two meltdowns at the grocery store and the three at the park, between the fifth and fifteenth times I asked him to put his shoes on, between the sixth and seventh times I asked him to stop screaming in the restaurant, the eleventh and twelfth times I asked him kindly to stop running in the house—my dream started to evaporate.

In that space between the five minutes of quiet I asked for and the thirty minutes it took me to do one task is where I lost my patience. Before I knew it, anger and frustration replaced my calm demeanor.

My gentle singsong voice was replaced by a voice that even *I* wouldn't want to hear. I'd become the mother I said I'd never be, bubbling with frustration and inner turmoil, overcome with anxiety and guilt.

There, in that moment — when I became someone I didn't want to be — the truth hit me. I understood just how human *I* was.

I'd been telling myself I was Superwoman, when, really, I was a regular woman doing my best in challenging situations. I realized that my natural tendency to become frustrated overtook my unnatural ability to keep calm through the chaos.

In that moment, I understood that patience is an unspoken superpower because it often means doing the opposite of what feels natural.

I know now that my patience isn't dependent on anyone but myself. Just like the skills my child is learning to master, patience is one I have the choice to master or let master me.

So you can imagine my surprise when the first few years passed, and my son proved to be just as human as any other child.

Patience is a practice that I want to access, especially when my natural response isn't calmness. I can create a space between my reaction and my response by taking ten deep breaths. I can lower my voice and increase the volume of my message. And I can ask myself, *What would I love to do?* and do just that.

Instead of anger and frustration, I can seek to connect rather than correct. I can put myself in my four-year-old's shoes to understand his perspective. In that space between the first hug and the fifth, between staring into his eyes and finding his sweet precious soul, I can see past his behavior and truly see *him*.

That is where I find my peace. And that is where I find my power as a mother.

When Anger Is All Too Real

MEGAN O'NEILL

Adjusting to motherhood was a huge shift for me. I felt my identity change and my marriage evolve. When I began to fully realize that my baby's life depended on me, the pressure felt overwhelming.

Cue my anxiety.

My postpartum anxiety (PPA) arrived on night one of my firstborn's life. I sat in the hospital bed nervously clutching him—wide awake and all alone in the middle of the night. The nurse came in to remind me about never putting him on his belly, but all I could hear was: "His life depends on you! How are you going to keep him alive?"

We headed home, and I never mentioned a word to anyone. I smiled, nodded when everyone told me how blessed I was, all while silently thinking, *What did I do? How can I handle this?*

After a few months of these anxious thoughts, I decided it would be good to spend time with other moms. At our "Mommy Meetup" we spent time chatting about motherhood, including the pressures, struggles, and joys. The anxiety lingered, but life went on. I worked out, found mom friends, started a new job, and slowly adjusted to my role as a mother.

Fast-forward to the birth of my third child, a girl after two boys. Everyone said, "She'll be so easy! She'll just go with the flow!" Since my children have never been the "go with the flow" type, I wasn't really expecting that to magically happen the third time around.

The first few weeks went well. I felt good and often thought, *Maybe I beat it this time! Maybe the anxiety won't come back.* But as we came out of the newborn haze and life went back to its hectic pace, I was yelling more and snapping at the littlest things.

I remember my son hitting the baby, and I yelled, "What are you doing?! Why don't you ever listen?" I squeezed his little arms and then immediately melted to the floor in tears, wondering what was wrong with me. *This* wasn't me. I'm a laid-back person. I have handled many stressful situations in my life with a calm demeanor. Why was I yelling?

This dual spectrum of worry and anger began showing up in many parts of my life. I often cried in the shower, feeling disappointed in myself. I was even losing my temper with my husband—the person with whom I'd started this family. I felt ashamed, like I couldn't do anything right. I saw myself slipping away but didn't know what to do.

One day I read an article about PPA that really hit home. It said that one of the symptoms of PPA was anger, along with a list of other symptoms (including obsessive thoughts, worrying, or feeling like the weight of the world is on your shoulders). I started nodding. *This* is what was happening to me.

But why doesn't anyone ever talk about the anger? I mean, it's embarrassing—I get it. No one wants to post a picture to their Instagram feed captioned, "Here I am screaming at my kids!" But it's real, and I'm forever grateful I read that article.

I decided to make some changes in my life.

I changed my diet, went to therapy, and finally spoke to my doctor. I decided to try medicine, which helped me tremendously. My anger lessened, my head was clearer, and the weight of anxiety on my chest was lifted.

I was ashamed to admit I needed medicine, but after noticing I felt better, I realized that it might not be for everyone, but it was the best choice for me and my family at the time.

I shared an article on Facebook recently about anxiety and anger and could not believe the response. Many women sent me a private message sharing their experiences. Others brought up the topic on playdates.

I am lucky to have had a support system of other moms who told me I would feel like myself again. I'm glad I can be that voice for other moms too.

You will be okay. And whether your help comes from yoga, therapy, or medicine, you can feel like yourself again.

Anger doesn't have to be present in your life all the time. Motherhood is stressful, but anxiety is not a prerequisite for being a mom. Pervasive negative thoughts don't have to consume you, and a quickness to snap doesn't have to last forever.

Create a support system around you. You deserve to feel happiness, and your family deserves the best version of you. *You* deserve the best version of you. We all have moments we are not proud of, but anxiety can bring out an anger in you that's surprising and disturbing. It's real, but it doesn't have to be your reality forever.

Editor's note: It's important for you to get help if you're experiencing post-partum anxiety, depression, or anger. If you don't know where to start, go to mother.ly/postpartum-help.

When You See a Tantrum

DIANA SPALDING

Dear grocery store onlooker,

It's me. The mom with the screaming toddler you saw in the store today. I wanted to take a few moments to talk to you. Even though I looked (and felt) totally out of sorts, the way you stared at me stung. I looked away so you wouldn't see my eyes well up with tears.

There were a thousand things I wanted to say, but my screaming toddler prevented me from being able to. But now he's tucked quietly into bed, and I'm ready to share some thoughts.

He's such a good kid.

That wasn't *him* today.

He was temporarily taken over by some powerful stuff, but in his core, he is so good. I know it's hard to imagine, but really, he's the sweetest, funniest little guy, and he fills my heart with so much warmth and happiness.

Tantrums are normal. Period. Every child has them, and it makes sense. My son has only been on this planet for two years and doesn't always know how to deal with his big feelings.

There was probably a good explanation for it.

He was hungry. I stretched him too far past his nap time. He's getting a tooth. Any one of those things is reason enough for a total meltdown. I know he made your shopping trip less pleasant. But I promise, he's not trying to give you or me a hard time. He's *having* a hard time. Big difference.

I'm on the verge of tears too.

I've been up since 5:00 a.m. I've already made three breakfasts (for the same person), done a load of laundry, attended a playdate, and gone grocery shopping. For the record, no one thanked me once today. I'm not trying to complain; I'm trying to explain. I love this job, but I am utterly exhausted, stressed, and full of self-doubt.

I don't know what to do, but I'm trying to figure that out.

I've read the books. I've Googled "how to deal with tantrums" fifty times (fifty-one after today). I've tried time-outs, ignoring them, hugging it out. But I feel totally lost. And kind of alone. If I could make it stop, I would. But I can't.

I love that kid so much, and I am trying to be a good mom. And I'll be honest, I think I'm doing a pretty good job. Perfect? No way. But everything I do comes from a place of love (and also a place of coffee), even when it looks like the scene you saw today.

Please don't judge me. Instead, look at me with compassion and speak kind words. It would make all the difference.

I am grateful to the people who have parents' backs. One mom made eye contact with me as I was leaving the store, smiled, and said, "You've got this." She threw me a lifeline when she saw I was drowning. And she'll never know how much that meant to me.

When I got into my car I started crying, not because of my toddler's tantrum but because of the kindness and solidarity she showed me. She reminded me that I'm not alone. Thanks to her, I'll have the courage to try again tomorrow.

Sincerely,
Toddler mama

Will It All Be Fine?

ANNE-MARIE GAMBELIN

I have three kids—one at home, one in college, and one who has graduated and is "adulting" in another country. It seems I've succeeded in safely shepherding them through their childhoods. I should be on the other side of that ocean of worry. But I'm not.

I think, as mothers, we worry. Period.

It starts when we decide to get pregnant. *Am I fertile? Am I healthy? Am I ready? Am I eating, sleeping, exercising, preparing, [you-name-it] enough? Will it all be fine?*

Every doctor's visit comes with its own set of concerns. *Is there a heartbeat? Is the baby okay? How do I do this? Can I do this? Will it all be fine?*

Once we have that beautiful baby in our arms, we hope our worries are over, but fear takes the lead. Without the buffer of a womb, it's even scarier. A tiny human is completely reliant on us to provide all they need. To do it "wrong" is to fail them.

Yet life is not about control. It is about faith—in our bodies, selves, partners, and love.

When I feared my youngest would never make it through a day of kindergarten without needing to call and hear my voice, I had faith my patient

To worry means
to know what
and how high
the stakes are,
and to care.

love would eventually give him what he needed to find his strength.

When I feared for my middle guy as his asthma sent us rushing to the hospital again, I had faith the doctors and nurses would know exactly what to do. And when my fear of his relapsing was so real that even I couldn't breathe, I had faith that I could handle whatever happened next. And I did.

When this same child was a newborn, I would quietly watch him sleep, to see that he was indeed breathing. He was. And in my sleepless stupor, I knew I was a good mama for the worry.

When my oldest disappeared as I turned my back at the museum, my heart stopped beating and the world stood still. I scanned the crowd, the doors, the stairs, only to spot her as her adventurous little spirit led her to the next exhibit. Her compassion for my tears upon finding her tempered her wanderlust for the moment. And I had faith that she would learn to think before she acted.

When this same child announced that she would move across a continent and an ocean to find her future, I feared that she wasn't old enough, wasn't savvy enough, wouldn't be safe. I worried that she wasn't ready—that I wasn't ready. But I'd done everything I could and had faith that I could let her go.

Will it all be fine?

To worry means to know what and how high the stakes are, and to care.

The fears we carry are not our own. They are as universal as the desire for our kids to be happy. As a mama with so many years of experience, I wish I could tell others that it *will all be fine.*

When you love your kids with all of your heart, they can't help but know it. That love in your heart and faith in yourself will be mirrored in the decisions they will make as they create their own lives. And they will be the good in humanity that you have brought them up to be.

That, mama, *is* fine.

Raising My Children In a Black and White World

ERICA L. GREEN

We want all the boxes to be checked. At first it's: Are they healthy? Yes. Happy? Yes. Sleeping well? Yes. Going to the bathroom regularly? Yes. Eating well? Yes.

Then it moves to: Are they making friends? Yes. Are they doing well in school? Yes. Do they really know who they are, where they came from? Yes. Are they proud of who they are? Yes.

When my babies' pudgy, pasty hands reached up to touch my face or laid upon my chest, the contrast was as stark as creamer in coffee. It was the source of running jokes, as they had my strong Afro-Caribbean features, but the paleness of their Jewish father, my husband.

We had made the choice to love each other for who we were — black and white — and create human beings who could carry on the ideals that brought us together, including how love transcends race.

We had encountered few barriers in our union as an interracial couple, and it was not lost on us that only a few decades ago we wouldn't have even been able to get married in some states. But in a century where the U.S. Census Bureau began allowing people to choose several boxes to identify their race, that all seemed like distant-enough history.

The month before I became pregnant, *National Geographic* published a powerful issue for its 125th anniversary that featured striking photos of caramel-colored children with distinctive and mismatched features—green eyes, kinky blonde hair, broad noses, and pink lips. The October 2013 issue boldly claimed that these children represented the changing face of America, where "race is no longer so black or white." So I often reminded myself, as I felt my baby girl grow inside of me, that I had a special part of creating this future.

But as I watch my little girl, now going on four years old, beautifully golden toned, with skin that lightens and darkens to reflect her father's and my coloring in the winter and summer months, I worry whether I was naïve.

We now live in a world experiencing a resurgence of racial divisiveness. White supremacists march in the streets. The leader of the Ku Klux Klan enthusiastically endorsed the president. Immigrants who match my daughter's skin tone are being called criminals. The countries of my ancestors are being degraded in the national discourse.

I worry that the boxes I had written off just a few short years ago as relics of the past will now define her future.

In recent years, the hashtag #blackgirlmagic has been a source of pride, but has also revealed a pain that my black sisters and I have suffered in silence—that we, as black women, have to be stronger, work harder to endure more, but earn less. My daughter, at least half of her, will undoubtedly learn that.

My daughter has a brother now, a fair-skinned boy with reddish undertones who may have a completely different experience from her. As I've watched black men gunned down by police on television in recent years, I wonder if the color of my son's skin will protect him against the same fate.

In some ways, I feel guilty—maybe I was overly optimistic to think that the love between my husband and I and the love we share with our children was enough, that the world was changing, and that somehow having two races would exempt them from being judged as one or the other.

What I've come to realize is, rarely is anything simply black *or* white. Raising children isn't. Motherhood isn't. My children's skin isn't.

And neither are the conversations we'll have to have in the future. I'm already planting the seeds for some of the bumps ahead. For example, every chance I get I tell my daughter that her curly hair is beautiful, especially when she asks for me to style it in a ponytail like the red-headed character in her favorite Disney show whose straight hair stretches down her back. When she mentions her brother's skin "looks like Daddy's" and hers "looks like Mommy's," I tell her how lucky she is that they get to have both. In those moments, the twinkle in her eye and her smile are reassuring, for she knows that to us—the people who matter most in her life right now—she is perfect.

My husband and I speak with our eyes during those conversations, silently acknowledging that the time is fast approaching when we'll have to shift the conversation to how having both of our skin may also bring some hardship. This will be especially true when the boxes begin to build around her and the cartoon characters she compares herself to become classmates, friends, and peers who influence who she is and how she sees herself in the world.

I am comforted knowing that we chose to live outside the box when it came to starting a family—and I do not regret it and never will—and we will raise our children to do the same.

As they get older, we will teach them to embrace all of who they are and where they came from: two people who loved each other, and who represent a world that is not black and white, but a reflection of deep love and hope for the future.

A Love Letter to the Baby I Lost to Miscarriage

AZIZAH ROWEN

My sweet angel baby,

Your due date was October 10. You were a "surprise." When I saw the two blue lines on the test stick, I was shocked, nervous, and excited. I felt a joy I had never previously experienced. I already loved you deeply, madly, immeasurably.

When we heard your heartbeat for the first time, we were giddy. We sat in the ultrasound room radiating with euphoria over your bold, fast, exquisite heartbeat.

We were mesmerized by the flicker of light—your heart beating in the center of your tiny shape.

The doctor said everything looked perfect and that you were healthy, so we started dreaming and planning for your arrival. We told friends and family. Presents started arriving. I stared at the little onesies, imagining you in them at a few months of age.

When the bleeding and cramping started, I had a bad feeling. My morning sickness had subsided, and my breasts were no longer tender. I have *never* in my life prayed so hard. I bargained with God. I asked him to *please* keep you safe and growing inside me. The doctor said I was probably fine, but instinctively I knew something was wrong.

One of the worst days of my life was the day I learned you were gone.

I stared at the sonogram technician's face and watched as a frown slowly crept over her lips. My heart fell from my chest through the floor because your heart was no longer beating and the flash of light was gone. *You* were gone. I felt like I'd been punched. The emptiness and pain were excruciating, and I knew I'd never be the same.

The hole remained in my heart for months. I was utterly heartbroken and walked around the busy streets of New York City feeling so alone. All I saw were pregnant women and children—reminders of what I could have had. I blamed myself. I was ashamed that my body let us both down.

I never realized how much I wanted you until I lost you. When you were inside me growing, I felt joy and hope and magic. Now every part of me ached.

One of the worst days of my life was the day I learned you were gone.

Weeks later I found out you were a girl. I imagined us together on our way to ballet class, a mommy and her little girl. I wept as I looked through my list of baby names for you. Women were made to have babies, so why couldn't I, when all I wanted in the world was to be your Mommy?

I wasn't sure I could go through the heartbreak again, but I couldn't stop thinking about you, so we tried again. Finally, we succeeded. Now I am Mommy to two beautiful boys. Motherhood has been everything I hoped for and more.

I still think of you from time to time, when October 10 rolls around or when I see stars shining in the sky. I imagine you floating through the clouds with angel wings, my heavenly baby whom I never got to meet.

You gave me purpose, and our experience together made me the mother I am today. You taught me about trauma and strength and hope. Your little light stayed with me and helped me forgive myself. You taught me perseverance. Most importantly, you taught me about love.

I will never forget you. You were not meant to be with me in this world, but you are an indelible part of me and always will be.

Love always,
Your Mama

The Autism Roller Coaster

JAMIE HENDERSON

The autism roller coaster is a ride you don't have the luxury to depart from. Once you have your ticket and board, you are on it for life. No returns, no exchanges.

Like many parents, I boarded the ride without even realizing it.

In 2013 I took my son to his pediatrician for his two-year checkup. She asked basic questions, and I could tell she wasn't happy with the answers I was giving her: No, he doesn't stack blocks. No, he doesn't turn his head toward my voice. No, he isn't saying any words.

While I was upset with her for making me feel like my son was broken, she was the only person who noticed that something was not right. So off we went for testing, then speech therapy, then occupational therapy.

I quickly realized that our family was on a different ride than I wanted to be on. I wanted our life together to be a smooth, fun ride full of laughs and smiles. This roller coaster started out with sharp turns and uncertain paths. At that time, I would have given anything to get off. But I couldn't. Instead, I needed to learn how to be the best advocate possible for my son.

Then in 2014, we were ascending slowly to the top of the roller coaster. We were at the specialist. My son was being assessed by multiple professionals, and finally they came into the room and said the words that rocked me to my core, "Jaxon has autism."

When hearing those words, no matter how prepared you are, you feel like you just hit the top of the roller coaster and you are plummeting down.

I was scared, nervous, and uncertain of how this ride would end.

Once we hit the bottom after finding out Jaxon's diagnosis, we started to move along the twists and turns of the system. As other parents of autistic children know, there are smooth parts that are fun and fill you with hope, and then there are the regressions—the gut-wrenching regressions where you don't know what you're going to do.

Like the regression my son had when he lost all of his words. I thought, *How could this happen? We've worked so hard and now it's gone?* I was feeling nervous and uncertain. Then, before I knew it, we were at the top of the roller coaster again when my son gained his words back (and then some).

Or the regression my son had when he became very aggressive seemingly out of nowhere. Aggressive toward me, his grandma, and his classmates. He had become a child who would push me and knock the breath out of me. He became the child who hit me in front of our family. I saw the shock on their faces before I left the room to cry. I was mortified. I became the mom who flinched when my child would run up to me. I was so tense that my body was sore constantly.

> You battle being stuck upside down for months until finally the roller coaster flips you back again—right side up.

You battle being stuck upside down for months until finally the roller coaster flips you back again—right side up.

The aggression disappeared, his vocabulary increased to where he could verbalize more, and we were able to communicate better.

Despite all the sharp turns and giant loops—this ride has also been filled with giggles, tickles, smiles, and love. So, so much love. But I have found that when we're riding the fun part of the roller coaster again, I'm watching and waiting. Waiting for the next flip or sharp turn. You wait for the next time you are stuck upside down and you prepare yourself. You build up your toolbox and get ready to help your baby when he needs it.

Even though this roller coaster has given us our fair share of unexpected twists and turns, there is such beauty in my son and our relationship. And after every setback and every meltdown, the milestones are that much sweeter.

The autism roller coaster is not a ride that anybody chooses, but it is the one we are on. While we're at the top, I will enjoy the view. While we're fighting our way through the bottom, I will use my strength to carry on, not only because I'm riding this very important ride on behalf of my son, but because I'm riding it alongside so many of you.

Motherhood Is the
Great Surrender

KELLY MAY

My first experience with anxiety and PTSD was at age twelve. September 4, 2001, my family and I visited the observation deck of the World Trade Center and a week later, planes flew into it. After that horrific day, I developed an unhealthy obsession with the news, and my anxiety spiraled out of control.

Eventually, I went to therapy and learned to deal with my anxiety on my own.

When I became pregnant, I thought I had the tools to manage my anxiety.

Two weeks later, my husband was laid off from his job, we lost our insurance, I was told I had gestational diabetes, and panic set in.

Next came morning after morning of nausea and vomiting, several breast biopsies after I found a lump, then a hospital stint due to a seven-millimeter kidney stone that was blocking my ureter and causing my kidney to swell at twenty-five weeks. After four days of pain, I underwent emergency surgery to relieve the blockage. I had to have nephrostomy tubes placed through my back into a collecting bag to further protect my kidney.

After this surgery, I remember crying to my midwife and asking if there was anything I could do—I felt *so* low. Things seemed to be spiraling out of control.

She looked at me, balled her hand into a fist, placed it into my open palm, and said, "This is your power. It's yours to have back."

It was a small gesture that made a big impact. I felt empowered, like I could get through this.

It was a hard transition, but I eventually got used to the tubes and bags. I had moments of sadness when my husband had to help me shower or I didn't know what to wear because not only was I pregnant, I also had these bags to disguise. Yet I continued to redirect my focus to the positive—my healthy child growing inside of me.

My child kept me going.

The tubes ended up causing more issues than expected. In total, I underwent ten surgical procedures while pregnant and in my first two months postpartum.

My experience was traumatic, but I refused to give up my power. Owning my power (mostly through prayer and therapy) while continually learning to surrender control has been a major theme throughout my pregnancy—and now new motherhood.

My faith has given me strength when I'm at my weakest. I know I can turn to it in the most overwhelming moments of motherhood. It won't be the same for every woman, of course.

You may choose art, yoga, writing, or meditation. Whatever it is, find something that can help you bring your awareness back to the task at hand.

> She looked at me, balled her hand into a fist, placed it into my open palm, and said, "This is your power. It's yours to have back."

The thing is, we don't have control over a lot of things. Our only real option is to take things as they come and figure them out as we go.

If you're a new mom like me, then everything is all-new. And what I've realized is that it doesn't just "click" immediately—for anyone—because we're all learning on the job.

Maybe control is overrated anyway. Maybe the illusion of control is actually holding us back from being our best selves.

Although it feels wildly unnatural to me at times, maybe going with the flow is a superpower in and of itself.

Maybe we should surrender—to the unknown, to the pull toward perfection, to the "shoulds"—and let the wind take us where it may.

Maybe when the waters get rocky, going with the flow is actually what will save us.

practice
FORGIVENESS AND SELF-COMPASSION

CAROLYN WAGNER

Self-compassion is one of the most important skills a mom can cultivate. It can see you through the rough patches that come along with the wild ride of motherhood and is a valuable skill to model for your children.

Self-compassion is the ability to recognize your imperfections without holding them against yourself.

It's the ability to see the whole picture, not *just* the part you wish had gone differently.

A good way to develop self-compassion is by writing a letter to yourself offering forgiveness. It can be centered on a specific incident you feel guilty about, or perhaps the fact that you're being too hard on yourself, or anything else that's troubling you.

Set aside fifteen minutes for this practice in a quiet, comfortable space where you won't have any interruptions or distractions. Bring pen and paper.

Start by doing some deep breathing. Bring to mind those instances when you're a strong, capable, loving mother. Allow yourself to enjoy the feeling of security and peace that comes from those images. Hold those feelings in your body and mind while you take four deep belly breaths.

Once you're feeling calm and relaxed, it's time to begin your letter.

Write to yourself as you would a friend who is struggling. Acknowledge the stress you are under, the difficult circumstances you're facing, and the fact that *no one* is perfect. (Because, truthfully, mama, we're all just doing the best we can.) What's done is done. Continuing to be hard on yourself won't magically wipe away the past. Only forgiveness can do that.

Let yourself know that it's okay, that you are forgiven. That you love your children hard and that you have the best of intentions for them at all times. That you are only human—a human who will make mistakes but who will learn from them and move on. That you are a good, good mom.

Make the letter as detailed or brief as feels right to you. When you are writing your letter, don't let it steer into negative territory. Remember to be kind to yourself. Be gentle with yourself. If you feel as though you're becoming negative, put down your pen and paper and revisit this practice again when you are ready.

When you feel you've completed your letter, put your pen down and take four more belly breaths. Then read your letter with an open mind and an open heart. Notice how it feels to be relieved of the burden of guilt.

Breathe in that feeling, noticing the lightness that comes with forgiveness.

Breathe in the sense of healing with the knowledge that at any point in the future, you can forgive yourself again for things that may come up.

When you've finished, fold up your letter and keep it somewhere safe but accessible. Reread your letter anytime you need to. Motherhood can feel heavy at times, and learning to have compassion for yourself will serve you well on this journey.

Remember, no one is perfect, and you don't have to be either.

journal
QUESTIONS

- How would you speak to a friend or family member experiencing the same challenges you're facing?

- How can you let go of negative thoughts and self-talk?

- How can you treat yourself with more kindness, with a more nurturing approach?

Simplify

Clutter is not just physical stuff. It's old ideas,
toxic relationships, and bad habits.

ELEANOR BROWNN

INTRODUCTION

JILL KOZIOL

Today's mamas are writing a new "back to basics" narrative, a backlash movement against all-consuming technology as a way to provide balance to our high-tech world. We often share articles on Motherly about minimalism, and we wrestle with how to raise creative children in the digital age. Today's mama is craving fewer things, less distraction, and more focused time with her kids and partner.

We want to let go of unnecessary "stuff" to make room for the beautiful things that suit our needs and our life.

I've always been drawn to simplicity and order—physical clutter around me causes my mind to feel cluttered too. Because my husband was in the navy when we first married and started our family, moving frequently taught me the beauty in simplicity and that children don't really need much to be happy.

When my daughters were two and a half and seven months old, we moved to New York City, squeezing ourselves into a one-bedroom seven-hundred-square-foot apartment. *Eek*. Looking back, I'm still not sure how we made it all work, but I *do* know that the apartment didn't feel cluttered or overwhelming.

We were intentional in what we brought into our home, especially "kid stuff." We made the choice, initially out of necessity, not to have a lot of toys and to spend our family time and money on experiences rather than things. We had the entire city at our fingertips, and our girls were always up for a trip to the American Museum of Natural History or the chance to scooter around Battery Park.

I know I'm not alone in this because Motherly's most popular video class topic is about decluttering and creating a simplified home. And our essays on letting go of the mental load of motherhood and returning to the basics are frequent top performers. As mothers, we want to be mindful and purposeful in *every* aspect of our lives.

I believe we are all yearning to let go of unnecessary emotional baggage. We carry so much on our shoulders. We set expectations that will always be just out of reach, chasing perfection. Previous generations had the "mommy wars," and we have Pinterest and Instagram, which often make us feel like we aren't enough. We hear that nagging voice inside our heads saying *You need to do more, have more, take on more. You need to be more!*

But here's a secret—we *are* enough, just as we are. There's no right way, and really, we don't need to please anyone but ourselves. We know our children and our families better than anyone else in the world and, at the end of the day, *we* control how we think.

Let's make a pact together to ignore that nagging negative voice inside our minds and, instead, let's listen to the voices in our hearts.

By doing so, we can truly simplify our lives and focus on what matters most to us.

We're redefining what we want our motherhood to look like every single day. We are in control, mama. What do you want to let go of in this season?

P.S. We designed this section to provide ways to help you free your life from clutter, chaos, guilt, perfectionism—anything that distracts you from your number-one focus of creating a happy family and a happy home. At the end of the section, we invite you to try our practice for letting go, which encourages you to be mindful of what you're holding on to that's no longer serving you, and be open to letting it go.

What If Hustling Isn't the Goal?

DENAYE BARAHONA

I spent most of my life in a hurry. My plate was so full that I had a hard time balancing it all. Straight up, I was doing too much. I was stressed and spread thin.

Then I had kids.

There's something about being a mother that makes you think you need to do everything. I spent the early days of motherhood doing just that: hurrying, hustling, and stressing.

Then one day, I stopped. I started to do less. I found calm. And I'm not going back.

I would love to say that it was yoga, mindfulness, or some other enlightened activity that brought about my sudden slowdown. It was when I wrecked a car. Three times.

The final incident was a brush with the iron gate in my driveway. It was my husband's car. To my surprise, he wasn't angry. He was concerned.

"You need to slow down," he said again. But this time his message carried more weight.

As a mother, my job is to set an example for my children.

For my children, I want calm.

I am not teaching calm when I live in a rushed, chaotic frenzy. I am not teaching calm when my train of thought is hauling a million pounds of freight on any given day. As a mother of small children, I know that "calm" isn't going to just spontaneously happen. That's why I gave up the chaos of motherhood in search of calm.

I knew that if I wanted to teach it, I'd have to live it. Slowly I started to unpack the overwhelm, which I'd spent years accumulating. These days I'm doing less and am confident it's the best thing for my family. I've finally found the calm that I want for my children. (And myself.)

> I am not teaching calm when my train of thought is hauling a million pounds of freight on any given day.

I worry less because I have realized that worrying steals my joy.

After I struggled through two miscarriages, I worried my way through a subsequent healthy pregnancy. When my first child was a late walker, I worried my way through several months of his sweet young life. Worry stole my joy—but it doesn't anymore.

I hustle less because the *doing, doing, doing* stressed me out.

Honestly, my hustling days are over. I have scaled back our schedules so we don't have to be someplace every moment of the day. Now I have more time to authentically connect with my husband and children. Today, stress and anxiety are at epidemic levels even for young children. It's important to me that my children have the rest they deserve to grow and develop.

I hover less and, in turn, am instilling a sense of confidence and independence in my children. My kids are learning how to fall.

My job is to kiss the boo-boos, not prevent them. My children are capable, and my actions communicate that to them. I will let them fall so they can learn how to get back up and try again.

I buy less; I quit filling our house with stuff.

I used to have a closet full of clothes I never wore. My kids had toys they never touched. Now we are conscious consumers who protect our home and credit cards against the accumulation that pervades today's society.

I interfere less because I can't solve all of their battles.

I won't rob my children of the opportunity to practice doing it for themselves. I love watching my kids problem-solving and working through disagreements with each other. I love seeing how capable they are without me sticking my nose into their business.

I gave up the battle of the what-ifs and the to-dos and traded them for a calm life that is infectious in the best kind of way. And this is my official invitation for you to do the same.

The Season for "No"

JILL KOZIOL

I hate to say no to people. I'm a firstborn daughter, so perhaps it's just in my DNA to be a people pleaser. I value feeling competent and capable. And, truthfully, I love saying yes. I'm ashamed to admit that it deeply validates me. I love the "I don't know how you do it!" comments, the recognition that I'm the kind of person who gets things done.

As a new mama, I said yes to it all: music classes, playdates, workout challenges, new work projects, the church bake sale, a spectacular first birthday party, date nights with friends, and Pinterest DIY projects.

I said yes, yes again, and then yes some more. As my daughter aged up to preschool, I learned there was always more to say yes to—like being class mom, chaperoning the class trip, volunteering for lunch duty, decorating for the fund-raiser auction, cofounding Motherly, leading my church's mothers' ministry, hosting playdates, and attending every book club and party.

Do you know what happened? I'm sure you do. I burned out.

My personal tank was on empty because I'd left no time for self-care. I was doing so much for other people, continually putting myself last, until my body screamed uncle.

I developed temporary blind spots in my right eye and was diagnosed with multiple sclerosis (MS). I was rocked to my core and was forced to reevaluate everything—from my career to family dynamics, my support structure, and wellness habits—including how often I said yes to everything except myself.

Thankfully, my amazing doctors think I'm very likely to never fully develop MS, and my disease hasn't slowed me down *at all*. But I have learned a few important lessons on taking care of myself because of my diagnosis.

Caring for ourselves is not selfish.

> Caring for ourselves is not selfish.

Repeat after me: Self-care is not selfish. Prioritizing your health and wellness as a mother does not make you a bad mom. It makes you a smart, empowered mom who is setting a good example. It makes you a happy and fulfilled mom.

Mamas, we have to be the ones to make it happen, especially in the busy seasons of motherhood. Accept your limitations, accept that you don't need to do everything at the same time. Some seasons, like the newborn one, you'll want to hunker down. Other seasons, like when you start a business or a new job, you'll want to be more career focused. When your children gain some independence, your season for volunteering may arrive. Empty nester? It may be your season to discover a new hobby.

With each new season comes new constraints and new opportunities. It may not be your season to be class mom or make home-cooked meals every night. Instead, it may be your season to volunteer for a monthly lunch-duty shift and schedule a meal-delivery service. That's okay—there will be a season for the other stuff, I promise.

There's a season for everything, including saying no.

Asked to chair a new committee? A perfectly reasonable response is, "I love the work you're doing, but it's just not my season to volunteer outside the home right now." A wise mama in my village recommends avoiding the automatic yes by responding, "Thanks for asking. I'll think about it and get back to you." What genius!

Responding this way has been life changing for me. It has afforded me the grace of self-reflection to prioritize my life around the things that mean the most in my current season.

And here's a secret: The requests won't end. There's no need to suffer from FOMO because there will always be another opportunity to say yes. And when you have the ability to say that yes wholeheartedly, it will truly be worth your time.

Easy Like Sunday Morning

CATHERINE DIETRICH

There's *no way* Lionel Richie could have been a dad when he wrote the ever-popular "Easy Like Sunday Morning." Because when you have young children, "easy" isn't quite the word that comes to mind when you think of weekend mornings.

There's nothing *easy* about being awoken by a two-year-old jumping on your head at 6:00 a.m. or about rounding up tired children for Saturday-morning ballet, soccer, or piano lessons before the sleepies are out of their eyes.

There's nothing *easy* about a family weekend day out.

Not when you're the one packing the kids' snacks, finding their shoes, wrestling them into their jackets, and assuring them that the outing is going to be awesome despite their protests that they don't want to go. Not when you're yelling, "Just get in the car—NOW! Please? It's going to be FUN!" Not when you feel guilty as you and your husband sit in stony silence and the children sniffle in the back seat.

There's nothing *easy* about kids' birthday parties, which seem to roll around every second weekend. I'm always wrapping gifts at the last second, unearthing directions from the depths of my email inbox, and making arrangements for the siblings, who'll be enjoying a sugar high when it's all said and done.

There's nothing *easy* about rushing from one social obligation to another so we don't offend anyone by declining an invitation—at the expense of quality family time.

There's nothing *easy* about being the one who keeps the wheels turning so weekends are days they look forward to. Nothing *easy* about weekends at all, really.

Recently, as my firstborn struggled to keep her eyes open while doing homework at 7:00 p.m. on Sunday, I guiltily thought of Maggie Smith in *Downton Abbey* and her deadpan expression as she asked, "What is a 'weekend'?"

Enough! I thought. It was time to slow down.

My children are overscheduled enough as it is from Monday to Friday. On the weekend my husband and I want to make sure our kids get the rest they need. We see it as our job to remove excess urgency from their lives, to free them of obligation—for just two days. We want them to have the room for spontaneity, unpredictability, creativity, and—dare I say it—a healthy dose of boredom.

As parents, we could benefit from the exact same thing. As a stay-at-home mom who spends far too much time talking to piles of laundry and a dad who works long and demanding hours outside the home, we tend to jump at any opportunity to socialize on weekends. We try to do too much, we say yes too often, and then on Sunday nights we're cranky and exhausted and realize we didn't do any of the things we'd promised to do on our days off.

So we've set some new ground rules.

Weekends now revolve around one little word that has changed everything for us: intention.

Weekends now revolve around one little word that has changed everything for us: intention.

Now our weekends are as deliberate as any other day of the week, but the crucial difference is that a good portion of our "plans" involve doing absolutely nothing.

This doesn't mean that as Saturday morning rolls around we sit staring at each other and the walls. It simply means that we leave ourselves open to a little bit of spontaneity. A little bit of whimsy. A little bit of whatever we fancy.

We've let go of saying yes to everything we were invited to do or felt obligated to do and instead we've said yes to slowing things down.

And you know what? It feels good.

It's a process—and we're not quite there yet. But I'm confident that one day soon, with a little more intention and a little less activity, our weekends will actually feel a little closer to being "easy like Sunday morning."

Mama, Stop "Shoulding" All Over Yourself

JILL KOZIOL

Ever since I can remember, my life was dictated by "shoulds" and "supposed to's."

I *should* get good grades. I'm *supposed to* wear the right clothes. I'm *supposed to* get into the right school. I'm *supposed to* get the right job. I *should* date the right guy. I'm *supposed to* be busy, always pushing myself, always improving. I *should* never settle.

So I went to the right school, got the right job, married the dream guy, and even got pregnant quickly. Little did I know, the "shoulds" were just getting started.

Now I *needed* to . . . find the right doctor, gain the right amount of weight, be Zen and peaceful, work out, eat the right food, design the perfect nursery, register for all the right things, and give my child the perfect name.

When my miracle arrived—unencumbered by all the "shoulds"—I went into overdrive.

I was overwhelmed with the pressure I put on myself to know exactly how I was *supposed to* instantly be the perfect mother.

I was *supposed to* . . . breastfeed, be an attachment parent, read all the books, be a sleep trainer, take time off work, go back to work, enjoy every moment, and take the perfect pictures and post them on social media.

And since I was the first of my friends to have a baby, I felt I *should* set the "right example."

As my daughter grew, the "shoulds" did too, and they started to affect my sweet girl. I'm *supposed to* pick the right preschool. I *should* sign her up for developmental activities. She *should* talk early. She *should* walk early. Our family *should* attend church and have amazing stress-free family vacations. We *should* have a sibling at the perfect time to ensure a close relationship.

I was so focused on doing everything I was "*supposed to*" and "*should*" do that I didn't listen to my heart.

When my second daughter experienced a health scare, I was rocked to my core, but it taught me to finally trust my instincts. Now, instead of saying yes to the "shoulds," I listen to my children, set boundaries for myself and for them, and hold on to my identity.

I realize that the best gift I can give my daughters is the example of a healthy, passionate, integral, fulfilled person who knows who she is despite all the expectations of what's "right."

Motherhood, ultimately, freed me. I was able to see the importance of actually *being* my children's mother.

Now when I'm feeling overwhelmed and impatient, I recognize I've been taken over by a "supposed to" pattern. This awareness has helped me learn that I don't need to be all the things to all the people all the time. It's imperative that I model confidence and authenticity to raise confident and authentic daughters.

I want my girls to have the freedom to discover the beauty of their own individuality, their own path. They can learn this through my self-reflection, modeling, love—and learning from their own choices.

So let's stop "shoulding" all over ourselves and our children and start living our lives like the precious, awe-inspiring gifts that they are.

Mothering Without Apology

EMILY GLOVER

You know those parenting moments when you're trying to impart an important lesson on your child and you end up having a revelation of your own? Something that causes you to pause and rethink how you've been doing things all along?

I just had one of those.

Here's the background: My husband and I have been working on manners with our two-year-old: Say "please" when you want something. Say "thank you" when you get something. Say "I'm sorry" when you do something wrong.

Our big-hearted toddler caught on quickest to "I'm sorry." Maybe a little too quickly—as he soon began apologizing each time he felt sad.

"Sorry, Mama," he'd say while trying to fight back tears.

"You have nothing to be sorry *for*," I'd reassure him.

It was like a lightbulb went off in my head because I knew exactly where he picked that up.

I could immediately think of a dozen times probably from the past week alone when I basically apologized just for being a person who *feels* and *needs*.

I was sorry I was asking for help. I was sorry for feeling so tired. I was sorry for worrying so much. And so on. The irony is, if it were my son I was talking to, I would praise him for seeking help when he needed it, for working so hard, and for caring so much. I admire these traits in others, so why was I feeling guilty about them in myself?

Somewhere along the way, "I'm sorry" had become my instinctual response for every occasion, from "I'm sorry I'm running late" to "I'm sorry you're seeing me cry."

But I don't want my children to ever think I'm inconvenienced by their feelings.

Why not let go of unnecessarily apologizing and embrace heartfelt gratitude instead?

Yet there I was, sending them the message that my own displays of emotion were shameful. And it isn't just me. As one study published in *Psychological Science* put it, women have lower thresholds for what they consider to be "offensive behavior" and therefore feel the need to apologize more often than men (Karen Schumann and Michael Ross, "Why Women Apologize More Than Men," September 20, 2010). While there is no study looking at how this behavior evolves during parenthood, I'm going to go out on a limb and assume mothers apologize more than just about anyone.

Between the guilt we carry with us on a daily basis and all the complicated emotions that get wrapped up in parenthood, this all can feel pretty messy. And when the mess spills over and touches the invisible boundaries of other people's lives, it can *feel* like we're doing something wrong—when, in fact, we're just being human.

By expressing regret over normal displays of emotion, we're not only teaching our children that they're exhibiting some kind of "offensive behavior," but we're also diluting the value of "I'm sorry" in the cases when those words really should apply.

Therefore, I'm vowing to pause before I rush into an apology and consider whether those are really the right words. More often than not, I'm finding they can be replaced by two others: "Thank you."

"Thank you for waiting on me. I know your time is valuable, so I really appreciate your patience."

"Thank you for being understanding that we're having leftover pizza again."

"Thank you for giving me a few minutes to unwind."

Although this difference is subtle, it's *significant*. For when we say sorry, we're asking for forgiveness. When we say thank you, we're showing appreciation without asking for a return. This is the kind of acknowledgment that often goes unsaid amid the chaos of life. (Goodness knows I haven't been telling my husband thank you enough lately.) Why not seize this opportunity to make others feel good about themselves?

Why not let go of unnecessarily apologizing and embrace heartfelt gratitude instead?

This doesn't mean the words "I'm sorry" are going anywhere. I *do* want my children to see that I'm not too proud to apologize when I've truly done something wrong, like those times I've said something I shouldn't or when I've snapped. I also want them to know the difference between true offensive behaviors and those that are simply part of a *true* human condition.

After all, knowing there is safety in loving relationships is what family is about. That means giving each other permission to feel the fullness of being a human in this world and everything that comes with it—no apologies necessary.

Getting Rid of Stuff
Saved My Motherhood

ALLIE CASAZZA

I was struggling.

I thought I was the only mom in the world who couldn't get it together, who wasn't really enjoying motherhood. I felt terrible. I sat on my couch with a giant pile of laundry next to me. Another day had come and gone, and I had barely been able to keep up. The days were flying by me, my kids were all four years old and under, yet I felt I had missed what childhood they'd had so far.

I was always cleaning up — and I was always falling behind.

When I thought about my days and how I spent my time, all I saw were dishes, an endless amount of laundry, and so much picking up — picking up toys, books, markers, jackets, shoes, empty water bottles, and paper artwork.

I thought I'd get to enjoy my kids when I became a mom, though I never spent time truly *with* them. I had to keep moving or the house and the day would collapse. When I did press pause and spent some time with my kids, it felt like I had to pay the price — catching up on housework, putting things away, helping us stay afloat amid the chaos.

After another particularly difficult day, I reflected on how I'd yelled, how I'd been the mom I never wanted to be, and how I was counting the hours of peace and quiet before morning came and I'd have to start over.

My life didn't feel abundant; it felt overwhelming and depressing.

In that moment, I had had enough. I decided I wasn't going to let this be my life, and this overwhelm wasn't going to rule me any longer.

What I did next set my life on a new course, and it never went back to the way it was. It changed everything.

I went into the playroom—the room that was the bane of my existence—and there were toys everywhere: on the floor, in chests, in boxes. It was too much. I started working through the room, making piles—keep, trash, or donate.

I got rid of every single toy I felt wasn't benefiting my kids.

If it didn't cause them to engage in constructive or imaginary play, it wasn't staying in our house because it wasn't worth the work it caused me.

If I was going to clean up, I'd save only the things that added to our lives—the things we absolutely needed and the things we truly loved.

When I was finished, all that remained were trains and tracks, a couple of dress-up costumes, books, and blocks. The trunk of my car was overstuffed with toys to take to Goodwill, my playroom was purged, and I immediately felt lighter.

The next day my kids ran downstairs for breakfast, and as usual I sent them into their playroom to play, curious to see if meltdowns would ensue because of what I'd done with their toys. They walked in, looked around, and said something along the lines of "Hey! It's nice and clean, Mommy! Hey! There are my trains!" and happily started playing.

I was shocked. I stepped out of the room, poured myself a cup of coffee, and sat on the couch. To my surprise, my kids played in that room that day for three hours. Three hours!

They started going outside more often, making up stories and scenarios together, playing tag, and creating art.

It was as if I had unclogged their God-given gift of imagination when I got rid of their toys.

I took my purging into other areas of the house—the dishes, the clothes, the drawers and cupboards—and our entire home life continued to transform. Without all of the stuff to keep up with, I spent less than half the time cleaning up my house. I played with my kids and took up homeschooling. My marriage even improved because I wasn't so cranky anymore.

Life felt lighter, more intentional, and I was no longer just "getting through it." This is what abundance in motherhood felt like.

I believe stuff is the cause of an epidemic of stress for today's mothers. Our stuff is literally stealing away our joy and our lives. It's stealing the most precious thing in the world—our motherhood.

Joshua Becker, founder of the website Becoming Minimalist, said, "Minimalism is the intentional promotion of what we most value, and the removal of anything that distracts from it." I believe mothers need minimalism more than anyone else.

Minimalism is less cleaning, it's the joy of always being ready for company to drop by without stressing out, it's more free time to focus on your priorities, it's enjoying your home rather than being owned by it, it's being able to be a mom who plays instead of always cleaning up. It's being a happier person.

I want this for you, sweet friend. You can choose a different path, you can thrive, you can love this life, you can escape the chronic overwhelm that everyone else calls normal.

Less is so much more, mama.

See Yourself the Way
Your Child Sees You

RASHA RUSHDY

I organized a playdate for my four-year-old yesterday, and I have to tell you—I went *all out*.

Normally, it's cut fruit and kids tearing the house apart while they play with the toys we have lying around, but yesterday? Oh, *yesterday*. I premade cookie dough, chilled it in the refrigerator like you're supposed to if you're an organized baker (which, most certainly, I am not). I made royal icing—from scratch—and not only that, but *six different pastel shades* of it, evenly distributed into six little piping bags, ready for small hands to decorate the cookies they were going to cut out and bake.

I was proud—I'm not even going to pretend that I wasn't. I was proud of the amount of thought and preparation and creativity I had put into organizing this cookie-making activity for my daughter and her two best friends.

I was so proud, in fact, that I sent a photo of the setup to my own mother to tell her so. She responded, jokingly apologizing that she had never provided me with such "high quality" childhood experiences.

And you know what? That got me.

I immediately told her that that wasn't what I meant, that I'd had an incredible childhood and still remember, frequently, the hundreds of things she did that made my childhood feel quite magical.

What struck me was, even though she was joking, I realized that although I'm now an adult, in my thirties, raising children of my own—my mom still didn't quite see herself as a mother in the same way that I, her daughter, saw her.

And so now, I'm going to ask *you*: How do you think *your* child sees *you*?

That birthday cake you cobbled together at the last minute? The one that leaned slightly and had frosting smudged all over the plate despite your best efforts, your mistakes embellished by the sprinkles you scattered on top? The one you brought out to the table with a sheepish grin on your face because it probably wasn't your best work?

That was possibly the most delicious cake your child has ever tasted, and she'll grow up and wish she could re-create a chocolate cake *just* like the one her mother made for her sixth birthday. Sprinkles, smudges, and all.

That maxi dress you throw on multiple times a week, the one you cringe at a little because there's that tiny hole near the waist you hope no one will see, the one whose colors are fading and whose style is dated, but it fits and it's comfortable and it *gets* you?

Your son's memories of his mama being the most beautiful woman in the world may well be a vision of you in that very same dress.

The five squadrillion activities you planned during your children's school breaks? The trips to the zoo and the aquarium, the badminton lessons, the movies and the crafts—*oh, the crafts*—the things you painstakingly researched and coordinated and scheduled?

Don't get me wrong, your kids probably loved them, and it's not to say you shouldn't do these things. But honestly?

I'm willing to bet that some of their favorite memories of school breaks will be the ones of you sitting on the floor with them while you played Monopoly or Go Fish.

Or when you laid together on the carpet while the early evening sun dissolved peacefully across your faces and you read that tattered old storybook—the one they secretly felt they outgrew but will read to their own children one day and hear your voice narrating those words every time.

You know how there was that tantrum you didn't defuse with grace and composure? Or what about the boundary they tested that pushed you beyond your limits and made you snap? Or perhaps it was the television you plopped them in front of because you just needed a minute to regain your sanity or get some things done without interruption?

What about all of those things you run through when you lie down at night, racked with guilt and promising to do better tomorrow?

Mama, if you only knew that what really stays with them is the hug you wrapped them in afterward or the gentle way you always knew how to wipe their tears and make them feel safe and secure. Or their awe at the fact that you manage to do *so* much for *so* many other people and still have loads of time, energy, and love for them.

I wonder sometimes . . . what would happen if I shifted my mindset with my own children to the one that I have of my mother?

I wonder sometimes . . . what would happen if I shifted my mindset with my own children to the one that I have of my mother?

What if I took a step back and simplified motherhood for myself?

What if *I* remembered that the things *they'll* remember are so very different than the things I *think* matter?

What if, when they grow up, when they have children of their own, the things I think are inconsequential, humdrum, routine, or no big deal are the things that will flash across their minds every time they encounter something that sparks a memory or when they perform a certain task?

What if, while you're worrying about all the ways you've fallen short or all the things you couldn't do or provide for your kids, they're busy adding all of the little things you do, every day, onto the stockpile of memories of their incredible, selfless, creative mom? The one to whom no one can compare and the one who is the *only* ingredient they needed in their childhood to make anything magical?

What if you simplified motherhood, mama? What if you took some of that pressure off? What do you think might happen?

I think you might be surprised at just how extraordinary that simplicity could be.

practice
LETTING GO

RACHEL GORTON

It's not uncommon for our days as mothers to be filled with heaviness and overwhelm. We have a list of to-dos, clutter that fills our minds and homes, and a whole lot of responsibility.

Maybe you feel like your life has become too full of tasks or you're constantly feeling exhausted by the emotional labor that comes with motherhood. Wherever you are in this moment, know that you deserve to give yourself the gift of simplifying.

You deserve to let go of what's bogging you down. You deserve to feel freer.

The intention of this practice is for you to give yourself permission to do just that—to let go.

We invite you to find a few minutes of quiet in your day—even just a few moments will do. Find a comfortable place and position, lie down if you'd like, curl up on a cozy chair, sit beneath the sun—whatever feels most nourishing to you.

Once you're comfortable, close your eyes and take three deep breaths. In and out . . . in and out . . . in and out. Allow yourself to feel calm as your mind quiets and your breathing slows. Meditation is not about eliminating all thoughts from your mind. It's about allowing the thoughts to present themselves, accepting and acknowledging these thoughts, and then letting them go.

Next, choose one or two of the following prompts to spend time contemplating.

Ask yourself:

- What experiences in my life feel most and least fulfilling? How can I restructure my schedule to create more space for those fulfilling things?

- How can I give myself a little more grace in whatever season I am currently in?

- How can I simplify our home to be more purposeful?

- In which moments do I feel the most self-doubt or self-inflicted guilt? How do I want to feel in these moments instead? (Set an intention or mantra to return to when these feelings arise.)

- What do I find myself apologizing for? What is another, more nourishing way to respond in those moments?

- What are the reasons my child would say I am the best mom? Where am I excelling?

Consider giving yourself one to two minutes each day to notice and celebrate the ways you are rocking motherhood. Come back to this practice any time you are feeling that heaviness of motherhood, and use whichever prompt speaks to you at the moment. Give yourself what you need in order to let go of burdens and embrace simplicity.

Remember, mama, things that could weigh you down will *always* be there, but you don't *always* have to let them.

As you work on letting go, you start to experience what life truly has to offer. You start to find contentment in this sense of spacious simplicity. In the beauty of fewer toys. In the wonder of seeing yourself through your child's eyes. In the magic of filling up your own cup. It *is* possible to let go of the negative feelings that you carry with you. And it *is* possible to find the joy in this beautiful journey of motherhood.

journal QUESTIONS

- Do you feel like you're rushing through life? What is one change you can work on to encourage a slower, calmer day-to-day?

- Do you find yourself holding on to negative thought patterns or physical clutter? What can you let go of today?

- Do you find yourself craving time away from social media? If so, what do you think the reasoning is behind that? If you use social media, how can you utilize your channels to engage with people in a meaningful way?

Strength

It doesn't get easier, you just get stronger.

ANONYMOUS

INTRODUCTION

LIZ TENETY

I once asked my mother who the happiest people she knew were, and we both agreed—they were my two grandmothers.

Both were the primary breadwinners of their families—one as a waitress, the other as a teacher—after their respective spouses became ill. One was widowed in her forties after her dashing husband died from complications of type 1 diabetes after more than a decade of blindness. My other grandfather was permanently disabled after a brain aneurysm.

Both women endured tremendous burdens in their lives as women and mothers. And both were full of more joy, empathy, and curiosity than you could imagine.

I believe they were this way not in spite of their hardships, but because of them. The burden of responsibility, so heavy on their shoulders, grew muscles of strength and determination.

Experiencing so much pain caused them to develop empathy deep within their bones. What they endured pushed them to embrace joy wherever they found it.

That's motherhood for you.

Sometimes your burdens look like a pile of dishes in the sink and a house destroyed by toys and a pile of laundry so tremendous you swear your home will not be clean for another twenty years.

Sometimes your burdens look like the uncertainty of a prenatal diagnosis and the ineffable, desperate prayer that goes up as you wait for more news.

Sometimes your burdens look like trying to work on deadline during a snow day when your kids are home with you and one of them has the stomach flu and you're just trying to survive until bedtime.

Still, you carry on. Tired, fierce, determined. *Like a mother*.

My hope for you is this: May your burdens do so much more than weigh you down. May they remind you just how strong you are because you're carrying a heavy weight on your shoulders and a lot of worry in your heart. But you're doing it every day, and you're an inspiration to those around you. And you are strong. Incredibly strong.

Like a mother.

P.S. We've included a practice at the end of this section to help you create a vision board. This fun activity will support the goals you have for your future, celebrate all your many strengths, and help create the intentionality you want to bring to your everyday #momlife. So, go grab your scissors, glue, and old magazines—it's (no pressure, nonjudgmental) craft time!

ALL Birth Is Beautiful

DIANA SPALDING

I *think* I've discovered why I love being a midwife and a writer. Before there was social media or TV and movies, there was simply the narrative. A group of people sitting together around a fire, sharing wisdom and tales.

Giving birth is the greatest adventure to ever be told. It's the culmination of your life's journey, the crescendo of the song your ancestors have been singing for generations.

Birth is the *ultimate story*. About power. About bravery. About hurt. About love. About becoming a mother. And mama, your story is breathtakingly beautiful.

The beauty of a birth story isn't in the details of how the birth unfolded. That would mean that each labor and delivery is somehow assigned a *level* of beauty based on some predefined criteria. Are the flapping of a bird's wings more beautiful than the sound of thunder? Is a fresh coat of snow more beautiful than the smell of autumn's leaves? Each of these wonders, like the details of your birth, are beautiful not in comparison to something, but in their own right.

This is not to say that the details of your story don't matter—they matter immensely. How you feel about your birth—*and all its details*—matters.

If your birth didn't go the way you wanted, it's okay to grieve. Cry big tears, hug yourself, and *be in* your disappointment that your story caught you off guard and threw you for unexpected twists and turns. But please, *please* don't be disappointed in yourself or underestimate the beauty of your story.

Your particular birth story is beautiful simply because it *was*.

Every contraction.
Every push.
Every minute that passed in the operating room.
Every hour you held your surrogate or partner's hand.
Every second spent waiting for your baby's first mom to deliver your child.

All bringing you closer to the moment of absolute transformation—motherhood. Because when a baby is born, so too is a mother.

A moment happens at every birth, vaginal or cesarean, medicated or unmedicated, just before the baby is born. Leading up to it, everyone present is just "doing their job." The mama is with her body doing its amazing work, the partner is supporting and encouraging, the midwife or doctor and nurse are analyzing and guiding. Then the room goes still.

The energy shifts to an almost reverent silence, if only for an instant.

From baby inside to baby outside. From woman to mother. A warrior is made.

A warrior who just grew a human inside her body.
A warrior who worried, sacrificed, felt ill, studied, and carried.
A warrior who gave her body over to the process of birthing her baby.
A warrior who now embodies the fiercest type of love.
A warrior whose heart is aglow and whose instincts are on fire.

> You, warrior-mama, are powerful.

A warrior who will, day after day, commit to doing everything in her power (and then some) to help her little one thrive.

A warrior who is the most beautiful thing on this earth.

Warrior-mama, there is nothing you cannot do now. Your strength is unparalleled. You will fight through the muck because you know that your reason to fight through it is worth it.

You, warrior-mama, are powerful.

Whatever the circumstances of your labor and delivery, you experienced the raw, vulnerable, and true presentation of one's soul to the world. All birth is beautiful. And you, warrior-mama, are beautiful too.

The Days Are Long, and the Years Are Short

COLLEEN TEMPLE

I've heard these words many times: "The days are long, and the years are short," and "Oh, it goes so fast!" And they're true—totally true. As I watched my firstborn baby zoom into preschooler mode, I marveled at how fast four years had gone by.

As a mom of three kids under four, I know that when you're in it, it can feel so slooooow.

Like, *it's-only-noon-but-I-feel-like-I've-lived-a-thousand-lives-today* slow.

By 9:00 a.m. I've negotiated a clothing debacle, broken up a sister skirmish, vacuumed the floor from the Cheerios incident, and nursed the baby four times.

By 10:00 a.m. I've heard my own voice at least six times asking my children to brush their teeth and put their socks and shoes (back) on. I've remembered to write out a check for soccer class, dug out the winter hats and gloves, added more diapers to the diaper bag, and washed the same load of laundry the third time to get rid of the mildew smell (again).

By noon I've gotten the kids into their car seats, fueled myself up on caffeine, settled the great snack debate, changed three diapers, sang songs at just the right pitch to please my tiny audience, soothed my crying infant, and answered fifty-seven questions.

I've also paused to wonder if I'm doing anything right.

If my children appreciate what I do for them. If my husband understands the rat race that is my daily life.

By 3:00 p.m. I've fed my children lunch, eaten something on the fly, picked up my daughter from preschool, signed up for parent volunteer slots, gotten my younger two kids down for naps, called the doctor back, and nursed the baby about eight times.

> As a mom of three kids under four, I know that when you're in it, it can feel so slooooow. Like, *it's-only-noon-but-I-feel-like-I've-lived-a-thousand-lives-today* slow.

By 4:00 p.m. I wonder where the energy will come from for the rest of the night. I wonder if I'm going to survive another two and a half hours until my husband gets home.

By 6:00 p.m. I've cooked and served dinner, I've broken up roughly ten arguments, found the baby doll that goes with the red dress, negotiated TV watching, and vacuumed (again).

By 8:00 p.m. I've had a twenty-minute chat with my husband, nursed the baby three more times, explained why one can't eat an entire bag of chocolate chips, watched a meltdown over the wrong pajamas, put toys away, cleaned up from dinner, put the recycling out, and added to our running grocery list.

By midnight I've soothed and nursed my baby (again), come up with tomorrow's to-do list, gotten water for my toddler, Googled fun activities to do, and managed to get some work done. I've fully exhausted myself (again) before finally going to bed.

In between all of the things, I've listened to a fair share of yelling, crying, and whining. I've been touched by someone at almost all hours of the day. Some days, by 3:00 p.m., I feel like it just needs to end. Some days there's too much asking, too much touching, and too much to do.

And yet, in the midst of what feels like constant doing and busyness, I'm often overwhelmed by the loneliness of motherhood too.

I am around people all day long, though somehow, some days, I still feel lonely... Sometimes I need fewer conversations with tiny humans about how Goldfish are the best snacks in the whole world, fewer debates about which song is actually the best from the *Sing* soundtrack, and more adult interactions (or, at the very least, a playdate).

The days are long, and the years are short.

Even though there's "too much" of a lot—there will never be enough hugs, kisses, laughter, and memories.

Those long days can be tough. But, mama, so are we. If anyone can handle these long, tough days, it's a mother. Mama, it's you.

As Strong as a Mother

KAYLA CRAIG

I define strength differently than I used to. I thought I was strong before I became Eliza's mom. I shouted the loudest and ran the fastest. I was managing a lot, doing a lot, being a lot of things to a lot of different people. But it turns out that's only half of what it means to be strong.

Now I'm a special needs mama, and this journey has taught me much more about strength and its many forms.

Quite honestly, strength has taken on a whole new meaning since my daughter came into my life. Eliza has Down syndrome and a rare form of epilepsy, which caused significant developmental delays. Most children her age can talk and walk, but I don't know when—or if—she'll ever do either. Yet as I look into my daughter's almond-shaped eyes, I see what it means to be mighty.

Strength is a multifaceted gem. It can be quiet and tender, such as when we appreciate the small victories, like reaching for a toy or maintaining eye contact. At times it's loud and bold, like when I advocate for my daughter's needs at her doctor's office or cheer her on at physical therapy.

As I comb Eliza's curls and rig up assistive toys, I'm given a chance to explore my own weaknesses and insecurities. I watch Eliza radiate joy. I see that I don't need to prove my worth to be her mother.

I don't need to question whether I am enough. I simply need to just *be*.

I'm learning to be gentle with myself. Motherhood has softened my sharp edges, revealing power in my weaknesses, magnanimity in my vulnerability. Motherhood has also deepened my *own* need for support, my *own* need for help in our day-to-day lives—and given me a newfound strength in asking for it. After all, moms need other moms. We're links in an unbreakable chain.

When seizures were taking over my daughter's body, women ahead of me in their special needs parenting journey helped me pinpoint what was happening and directed me to the best specialists. When a calendar full of therapy appointments felt like too much to bear, local mom friends encouraged me to keep going. They understood my journey in ways others couldn't. They understood the force behind a mama bear advocating for her child's needs.

I've watched countless women mother children with medical or special needs. They radiate a strength, resiliency, and beauty when adversity strikes.

Superheroes may be mythical, but mothers fueled by love for their kiddos are powerful beyond measure.

I just have to keep showing up.

Even with a village of women by my side, motherhood isn't easy. Parenting a special needs child teaches us that sometimes we *can't* fix things. Giving up isn't an option either, so we keep going, even when we don't know where the next step will take us.

Strength is putting one foot in front of the other, appreciating the beauty of what *is* instead of what *isn't* or what *could be*. I no longer look at my parenting in terms of victories and defeats—my children's or my own. Instead, I truly live in the present and give myself grace in everyday moments.

It's in these moments that I truly understand what it means to be strong. I can't do it all, and I don't have to. I just have to keep showing up.

And I will. I'll stand tall for my daughter. For my children. I'll make myself big when I need to, I'll fight for them, work to make the world better, more accessible, more accepting for them and because of them. But I'll find power in standing down too. Not all battles need to be fought today or this week or ever, for that matter, and I'll find strength in making that choice.

I'll be as strong as a mother, in all her beautiful forms.

I Am a Survivor, I Am a NICU Mama

AZIZAH ROWEN

I am a NICU mom. I became the one-in-ten statistic when I gave birth
to my warrior-baby, Wilder. I never thought he would be a statistic, but he
is one of the four hundred and fifty thousand babies born prematurely in
the United States each year.

His story is like so many other preemies' stories. Two months before
his due date, Wilder was born abruptly at thirty-one weeks. He spent his
first days on earth clinging to life, breathing through a tube, and living in a
small incubator. He spent a terrifying forty-nine days in the NICU before
I could bring him home—forty-nine days of ventilators, beeping alarms,
specialists, health complications, and endless fear.

**From the second he was whisked away to the NICU, we were in
survival mode.**

The first time I held him I couldn't believe how small he was. He weighed
only four pounds, the size of a pineapple. He had tubes coming out of his
mouth and nose and was hooked up to heart and oxygen monitors. I was
hysterical, sure that I would lose him.

Wilder's NICU staff comprised a dream team of the most incredible
nurses—all angels on earth. With effortless ease and loving care, they calmed

any situation, dried my tears, and reassured me that although my baby was weak and sick, he was in *very* capable hands. They didn't make false promises about an outcome they couldn't predict but were confident that his breathing difficulties and appearance were consistent with a baby born at thirty-one weeks.

Every day, a new struggle presented itself and my husband and I prayed that our son would survive. We vacillated between being terrified and inconsolable to strong and hopeful.

For the next two months, I had a routine in place and ran on adrenaline. I would wake up, spend time with my oldest son, and then go to the hospital to cuddle my second born all day until it was time to go home and sleep. I made NICU mom friends in the pumping room where we shared our fears and discussed our babies' "accomplishments," like when one of their feeding or breathing tubes were removed. We were surviving together, working toward one common goal: bringing our babies home.

Wilder's day finally arrived. In mid-March, he felt fresh air for the first time on his perfect little face. I'd been dreaming of that day for so long. Then, when it actually came, I was terrified. I remember wondering, *After surviving the NICU, would he survive the world?*

Thankfully, he did. Wilder is now four years old. He is beautiful, strong, hilarious, and fearless. He has a contagious laugh and a positive energy. I cannot imagine life without him.

To the mama whose baby is suddenly in the NICU: You are *not* alone. It's a complicated journey, but you will prevail.

You'll be stronger than ever before, and you'll be filled with gratitude for the doctors, nurses, and research scientists who make life possible for so many babies.

You may blame yourself for not being able to carry your baby to full term, as I did, but it's not your fault. I've come to accept that there was nothing I could have done to prevent him from being born early. I hope you'll do the same.

I am the proud mom of a small but fierce NICU baby, and I am a mother who survived the NICU experience. It wasn't a journey I would have chosen, but I've carried that strength with me every day since my son was born. Walking out of the hospital with a baby is a gift; walking out with a NICU baby is a miracle.

Preparing Your Heart for Baby Number Two

ERICA DESPAIN

A few months ago my two-year-old daughter and I were driving home from dinner with friends. As we pulled onto our street, a lump formed in my throat and big tears began to stream down my face. That night would be the last time just the two of us would do her bedtime routine. Out-of-town relatives were set to arrive, my husband was coming home from his deployment, and we'd soon be having our second baby.

The intense emotions hit me out of nowhere. I felt guilty because so much was about to change for my daughter.

I had no idea how to sort through this sudden rush of feelings. I was already so in love with my unborn baby girl in my belly, but I also felt I was mourning the season of being a mama of one.

Fast-forward three months later. A lump was in my throat, but this time it was from watching my two-and-a half-year-old daughter love on her infant sister. I had stepped out of the room for a moment, and when I returned I found my older daughter crouched down by the baby, wiping spit-up off of her face and making sweet baby talk.

As I watched my baby locked on to her sister's eyes, I recalled my emotions from a few months before. I couldn't begin to imagine *then* how full my heart would feel watching the two tiny loves of my life interact with each other. Even now, it sometimes takes my breath away.

I was so worried then about the unknown and making my daughter "share" the life we'd all built together, but it turns out we had nothing to worry about.

To the mama whose heart is currently twisted about going from parenting one kid to two . . . You'll never have to split your love between your babies.

You may wonder how it will be possible to ever love another little person as intensely as you love your first. But just wait, mama. Your love will multiply tenfold as you all get to know your newest little love.

It's *beautiful* and *perfect*, and it happens so effortlessly.

Try to remember that this is an adjustment period, regardless of how long it lasts. (Plus, your oldest may surprise you with how quickly they adjust.) You may mourn all the things you love about being a mom to one and worry you'll never get into another routine that's comfortable and easy.

I used to watch other moms who had two or more children and wondered if they could empathize with my roller coaster of emotions about adding another baby. They would move seemingly effortlessly through the grocery store or a restaurant with two or more little ones, and I remember hoping to be able to juggle multiple kids as naturally as they appeared to.

It's *beautiful*
and *perfect*,
and it happens
so effortlessly.

Trust me. You'll find that comfortable routine again (eventually), and this time you'll have the privilege of having another little soul to love and raise and enjoy.

If your heart feels conflicted about having your next baby, or this moment seems bittersweet and you're taken aback by the flood of emotions, know that your feelings are relatable, understandable, and justified. You may choke up like me when it's time to give your biggest baby one last hug before you meet your second one, but remember—this is all a part of this exciting adventure we call motherhood.

Your heart is about to grow so much fuller with love. You have a very strong heart inside you, mama. It is ready.

The Strength
of a Single Mom

SYDNEY HUTT

If you were to ask me about the hardest thing I've ever done, it wouldn't be carrying my identical twin girls or coping with their premature birth. It wasn't fighting suffocating postpartum depression or even deciding later to divorce the father of my children and move out on my own for the first time in my life.

It was when I became a single mother and *every* parenting and home life responsibility fell entirely onto my shoulders.

There was no one else to help tidy up toys or dishes, no one else to wrestle the girls into pajamas and tuck them into bed after a long day. No one else to fold the laundry, buy the groceries, or pay the bills.

In a once-longed-for evening of solitude, the silence felt physical and oppressive without a partner to buffer it. I realized that if my stress cup runneth over, I was the only one around to clean up the spill. For months after my decision, I wondered incessantly if I'd done the wrong thing—if I was permanently damaging my children and myself by forcing us into this strained existence, which I wasn't sure we could survive.

But we have. And we are surviving.

There's something beautiful in learning how much you're capable of.

I used to think my patience had a limit, but it became nearly inexhaustible once it had to. I found strength in big things, like balancing a budget alone, and little things, like taking out the garbage. I began to learn new things about myself. I found the joy of not compromising—of decorating our apartment in layers of pink florals, leaving dishes in the sink, and never having to share the remote.

Gradually, I began to discharge all the things I'd pressured myself to be perfect at when I'd been someone's wife. In the chaos, a sense of adventure returned to my life. There wasn't any other option.

Even holidays became uniquely wonderful. I'd previously spent most Decembers panicking about creating a flawless holiday. As a single mother, I found that what I could provide was more than enough. That first year our tree was fake, but our joy was real as my girls and I dug into hot gingerbread straight from the oven, melted icing dripping down our fingers.

And that winter I killed two giant spiders in our apartment all by myself, despite years of rampant arachnophobia. Afterward, I immediately texted my mom exultantly, and she replied, "Living alone is empowering because it isn't easy."

Nothing worth having ever is, is it?

If pregnancy and delivery teach us what our bodies are capable of, motherhood—and perhaps even more so, single motherhood—shows us that many of our limitations are malleable perceptions, capable of adapting to even the most challenging situations.

Despite the struggle of raising two children on my own without a full-time partner to help shoulder the weight (and the individual and social isolation felt because of that), I wouldn't change our journey.

After all, without single motherhood, I'd never have realized my capacity for endurance and gratitude. For me, this raw, flawed life satiates the soul more than a perfect family photo ever could.

After Infertility, I Am Free

JENN PRESS ARATA

Last winter, after I experienced a miscarriage, my husband and I were mourning the loss of our baby's due date while preparing for an IVF transfer with our final, frozen embryo. The ultrasound technician knew of my story and how I was literally putting all my eggs in one basket.

"That's your baby," she told me. She was right. It worked. After many scares throughout the pregnancy, our miracle son entered the world six-and-a-half weeks early. I suppose he didn't want us to have to wait any longer. After a few weeks' stay in the NICU with tubes in his nose and uncertainty in our hearts, we brought him home to begin our family of four.

He was *real*. He was *ours*. Our daughter was a big sister. We could *finally* exhale.

When I was given permission to return to exercise, a rush of adrenaline came over me at the thought of getting my body back, realizing that for the first time in seven years, it was finally mine. All. Mine.

Mind you, I'm not referring to working on a six-pack or anything. It was the relief of being done with fertility struggles *forever*. Pregnancy—and my journey to get there—equaled a long list of things I couldn't do. I was either gearing up to conceive, growing a baby, dealing with a loss, or postpartum. On a vicious, repeating loop.

Six losses and countless procedures later, I could finally celebrate knowing I'd never have to do any of this ever again. And it was incredibly liberating—luxuriously so.

After years of donating my body to science and childbearing, I'm finally taking it back.

If I want to work out daily, I can do it. I'm no longer high risk. If I want to tackle a juice cleanse, I don't have to worry about how it will affect my meds. If I want to gain some "happiness pounds" by serving up a plate of unpasteurized cheese, then bon appétit to me! I can do these things. The choice is *mine*. No more pills. No more needles. No more waiting. No more recovering.

I'm taking my calendar back too. No more trekking back and forth long distances to specialists during morning rush hour. No more planning social events around appointments. I'm filling my days with fun. With friends. With family memories. With laughter.

During this new stage of motherhood, I feel a new sense of adventure in me—a fire and passion burning inside again.

I've always had a zest and an energy; now I can embrace it with every sense of my being. No more wanting to run and hide. No more aching heart.

I feel complete and content and grateful.

When my husband and I went on our first date after becoming parents of two, it was about just *us* again. For the first time in ages, we weren't out to mask the pain; we weren't escaping. I wasn't holding back tears during our appetizers. We weren't discussing our next steps about when we were going to try again or tiptoeing around the subject sipping on a cocktail I wish I wasn't allowed to drink. This time, we clinked glasses to our happily ever after.

As a mother to my two miracle, rainbow children, I have the most responsibility I've ever had in my life. And yet, I've never felt so free.

We Still Show Up

RACHEL GORTON

My grandmother once told me, "Motherhood is hard, and there are days when you might feel like you can't do it. But as long as you show up, you are already halfway there."

Over the years I have realized how right she was.

There are so many moments when real feelings of defeat and failure surface, but there are also many moments when being a mom simply means: We show up.

We show up in the early stages of motherhood, which start before we even hear a heartbeat. We show up as we watch our bodies grow and change in preparation for the intensity of nurturing a human. We show up when we wake up from a full night's sleep still feeling tired, when we struggle to make it through the day without crying, and as we pull our pants over our swollen bellies before heading to work.

We show up after nine months of pregnancy or after months of waiting on an adoption list, ready to get that call—desperate to meet our little ones. Maybe we went through hours or days of intense labor dealing with pain we didn't know existed, channeling strength we never knew we had. Maybe our heart has been tested by previous situations falling through in our adoption journey. But we do it because we must. Because showing up means bringing new life into the world.

We show up when we have newborns and our days are spent feeding, changing diapers, attempting naps, and folding clothes — all while running on little-to-no sleep.

We show up during the chaos of toddlerhood, when our children need us to be present and patient with their ever-changing emotions.

We show up when we find ourselves in the school-age years and instantly become chauffeurs and meal coordinators, shuffling our own plans around sports schedules.

We show up when our kids decide they want to be ballet dancers or football players and are suddenly interested in juggling and Lego clubs before and after school.

We show up when life gets messy and complicated, and it seems our children no longer want to be around us. When somehow we've been replaced with friends they barely know and eventually love interests we may be less-than-excited about.

We show up when our kids are sick and we're sick too, but they need us. We power through to be caregivers to them first.

We show up when it feels like we aren't doing anything right, and we question every decision we're making.

We show up when all we really want to do is run away. When, on those days, we don't think we're cut out for parenting and wonder why we were given this job. But we *don't* run away. We *don't* give up.

As a mother, our heart can be broken and our confidence can be shattered — yet we *still* show up.

Being a mother isn't easy — in fact, it's likely the hardest thing we will ever do in this life. But even when we don't feel like we have it all together, our children are noticing all the times we show up. They *know* we are there for them.

The challenges of motherhood will always be there, and we might not handle them as gracefully as we'd planned or hoped. We may not know exactly what to do every single time. But the beauty of motherhood is that by just showing up during both the great times and the hard times, we are halfway there, mama.

CREATING A VISION BOARD

ERIN LEYBA

A vision board is a collection of words and images that represent your goals, passions, interests, and identity. It can be a powerful and inspirational tool to help you not only identify what's important to you but to focus on where your strengths lie and picture how you'll bring your vision to life.

Vision boards can include goals or intentions related to relationships, work, purpose, parenthood, self-care, spirituality, projects, leisure time, travel, health, or emotional well-being. Putting them together can help you answer important questions, such as *What exactly do I want my life to look like? What do I want to work on?* or *What do I want most out of motherhood?*

Research on the power of intention in sports, business, psychology, and other fields suggests that getting clear on *exactly* what you want and "putting it out there" to the universe helps you build it. A vision board can help provide the motivation you need to reach your goals.

Consider choosing one word, an intention that will be the theme of your board. Perhaps you'd like your mama superpower to be the ability to be truly present, regardless of what's in front of you. If so, focus your board around the word "present." If you want to feel confident about working with your partner to lay a foundation for your family's success—focus your board around the word "teamwork." Before you start your vision board, take some time to think about the goals you'd like it to reflect.

To create your vision board, you'll need scissors, glue, poster board, and magazines. It will take about one hour to create your vision board. Dedicate the first thirty minutes to brainstorming and gathering.

Spend ten of those minutes thinking about what you want for your future and what goals you're setting for yourself. Jot them down on a piece of paper or in a journal. Then take twenty minutes to cut out photos, words, and quotes from magazines or print out specific items you want to include. Use personal photos too. Dedicate the next thirty-minute sitting for assembling your board by gluing all that you've gathered onto it.

Your vision board might contain:

- **Positivity + Strengths.** Reflect on words or phrases that have positive meaning for you (e.g., "affectionate," "down-to-earth," "fun-loving," "warm," "funky," "easygoing," "vibrant," "eco-friendly," "strong," "compassionate," "nurturing," or "hardworking") and include them. Add uplifting quotes or mantras from books, articles, poems, song lyrics, or people you admire. What speaks to you most for this moment in your journey?

- **Goals.** Vision boards often match a long-term goal with a few simple and practical action steps. If your goal is to show your kids how happy they make you, you might match it with an action step like "Say something positive to each child first thing in the morning." If you have the goal of keeping friendships strong, you might put the action steps of "Attend playgroup once a week" or "Meet a friend for coffee once a month" on your board.

- **Images.** While words are important, visuals help us remember things more clearly because they're stored in our brains differently. Look for magazine pictures, photos, drawings, symbols, or any other beautiful and inspiring images for your board. Consider photos that depict what it would look like if you were meeting or had already met your goal (e.g., a photo of a runner, if you want to start doing 5Ks). What does strength look like to you? What about success? How can you represent your goals visually?

- **Identity.** Parenthood is challenging, and some days you may not recognize yourself. Use your vision board to identify the old and new aspects of your personality, values, daily life, and interests that are central to your core. What aspects of your pre-mom self do you not want to forget about? What do you really want to make time for now? What do you love about your past and present self? Where do you want to improve?

- **Joy.** Ask yourself, "Where will my joy come from this year?" Include pictures or words of things that will fill your days with peace, happiness, fun, sweetness, or buoyancy.

- **Gratitude.** Although vision boards traditionally focus on new goals, add at least one thing you're already thankful for (like a flexible job, loving grandparents, or a partner who makes you laugh) or at least one thing you're proud of. Celebrate your accomplishments, mama!

- **Compassion.** Include a word or an image that depicts compassion for yourself regarding the goals you haven't yet accomplished, the ways you feel like you're failing, and the areas of motherhood, or life in general, where you struggle most. Consider words and phrases like "patience," "let it go," "fully human," or "life's imperfect and so am I." Use a word or an image that will motivate you to extend kindness and forgiveness to yourself, like you do every day for your children.

journal QUESTIONS

- What are your mama superpowers?

- What are some obstacles you have faced and how have you overcome or learned from them?

- How do you envision your life one, five, or ten years from now?

- What example do you most want to set for your child(ren)?

Magic

And above all, watch with glittering eyes the whole world around
you because the greatest secrets are always hidden in the most
unlikely places. Those who don't believe in magic will never find it.
ROALD DAHL

INTRODUCTION

JILL KOZIOL

You know that moment when you check on your sleeping kiddo after a long day? No matter what kind of day you two have had, that moment always seems magical. You're glad because today was a doozy and they're finally asleep (*and* OMG look at how cute they are).

Sometimes it's hard to see the magic in the challenging moments of motherhood. It's hard to find wonder and joy when you're frustrated or bored. I get it.

As cofounder of Motherly and a voice for many women in motherhood, I sometimes struggle with imposter syndrome. I'm far from a perfect mother. I lose my patience, I make mistakes. I doubt myself. Neither Liz nor I have this all figured out, but we're in this together.

Motherly is about being okay with imperfection, with holding onto our core identity as we navigate this wild, amazing journey.

It's about realizing how magical motherhood is. It's about finding that magic on the hardest of days and on the most beautiful days too.

Changing the fourth diaper blowout of the day may not look like magic, but it's there in your ability to keep your baby clean and cared for and loved in a million little ways.

It's hard to see the magic at 3:00 a.m. when you're so tired that you worry you're going to fall asleep while nursing your baby, but it's there in your dedication to your family and in tending to their needs.

It's hard to see the magic when the teacher calls you in to talk about your child not being inclusive on the playground, but it's there in the gratitude you feel for such a caring, thoughtful educator.

It's hard to see the magic when it feels like no one is listening, but it's there in the patience you maintain *and* the grace you extend yourself when you, well . . . lose it.

Mama, I want to help you to see yourself like I see you—as a fabulous, strong, incredible, hardworking woman and mother.

I also want us to always remember how lucky we are to be on this journey and that we are truly in it together. Motherhood is hard and challenging, but it is astonishing too, isn't it? There's so much magic happening around us on a daily basis—especially in the little moments. I implore you to challenge yourself to find it when you can. And I will too.

That rare moment when you get out of the house relatively on time with smiling children? Celebrate it!

That random time your daughter decides to try the broccoli you've encouraged her to eat for weeks? Yay!

The sweet, clean smell of your little one as she climbs into your lap after bath time and melts your heart by saying, "Mama? I love you." Relish it!

These magic moments are what motherhood is made of.

I see the magic of you, mama. You are strong. You are brave. You can do anything. And I'll let you in on a little secret: Your child sees the magic too.

You've got this.

P.S. We've included a guided meditation at the end of this section to help you connect with the special moments of your motherhood journey—the ones you never want to let go of. Come back to this meditation as frequently as you need to. We hope it reminds you of the magic that is motherhood, especially when you need it most.

Don't Let Me Forget Their Littleness

RASHA RUSHDY

Here I sit on my bed, the toddler on my left and the baby on my right. They're fast asleep, peacefully dreaming of the things little ones dream about. If I listen closely, I can hear their steady, soft breaths and see their little chests rising and falling.

In this still, quiet moment, I beg the universe: Don't let me forget.

Don't let me forget the way my baby's fine, silky hairs tickle the tip of my nose as I breathe in her perfection, or the way she giggles as I bury my head into the cushiony folds of her chubby neck. She smells like milk, soap, and baby powder, even though I didn't put powder on her. She smells like love, hope, and some magical, mysterious ingredient that only babies possess.

Don't let me forget the gentleness of those soft, spongy, warm little hands.

The little hands that clutch me like I am everything she needs, that graze and bat at me when she wakes up too early and I put her next to me in my bed and try to steal a few more minutes of sleep. The little hands that reach up to touch my face while I nurse her. The little hands that linger and hold on to me, reluctant to release their grasp as I place her down to sleep.

Don't let me forget my superpowers.

My power to kiss away an ouchie, hug away sadness, hum away a bad dream, and soothe fear and worry. My power to know exactly what she needs when even *she* doesn't know. My power to calm her simply by being close.

Don't let me forget the weight of raising babies.

The heaviness of a drowsy head while she nurses or the feeling of a warm, tousled, freshly bathed head on my shoulder while little arms wrap snugly around my neck. The overwhelming power of this love between us.

Don't let me forget the sound of little feet on my floor.

Little feet running delightedly toward me. Little feet treading slowly into my room at night when my toddler is frightened by the thunder. Little feet squeaking on the tiles as she follows me around the house, wanting to do whatever *I'm* doing.

> Don't let me forget the beauty of my children's imaginations.

Don't let me forget this bond we have.

The way she fits perfectly onto the curve of my hip, as if it were designed just for her, or the way her strong, chubby legs kick excitedly as she watches what I'm doing while I sway her gently.

Don't let me forget the beauty of my children's imaginations.

The way my oldest pronounces certain words in her own unique way or the way she imitates my intonation or the sound of her singsong voice as she narrates one of her brilliant made-up stories. Or the games she invents and the conversations we have. The way we can make each other laugh.

Don't let me forget the small moments.

The way everything seems to glow as my precious ones and I lie in bed together on lazy mornings, while they roll around with each other and giggle and squeal, and I watch them, tiredly, proudly, gratefully, wondering by what stroke of luck these two were chosen to be mine.

Most of all, don't let me forget their littleness.

Sometimes their littleness makes me wish they would just grow up faster, sleep for longer, be more independent, give me more personal space, and let me just do what *I* want to do, for once. But it is that littleness—that precious, fleeting littleness—I will one day ache for and miss dearly.

So, let me bask in it a little bit longer, breathe them in a little bit deeper, and hold on to them a little bit tighter because soon this sweet littleness will pass.

But, please, don't let me forget their littleness.

Watching My Kids Love Each Other

DIANA SPALDING

I am a midwife. I've been there as many women met their second (or third or fourth) child. I saw mother after mother fall madly in love with baby after baby. So, when I was pregnant with *my* second (and third), I never doubted that I would love them as much as I loved my first. But I have to admit, I wasn't prepared for the heart explosion that happened when I watched my children fall in love *with each other*.

When our favorite creatures on earth, who we absolutely adore, recognize the amazingness in one another . . . well, it's just awesome. These moments—seeing this sibling love—happen in subtle ways and monumental ways, each taking my breath away and filling me with joy.

They protect each other.

Siblings are quick to go to battle with each other over a toy, but heaven help the kid on the playground who picks on one of them. They stand up for each other too. My eldest is quick to point out when I've been unjust to his younger brother. "Mooooom, you told him he could have a cookie when we got home from Target."

They are a squad. They truly want what's best for each other (except when the other one *has* a cookie; then it's every kid for themselves).

They teach each other.

They are constantly observing each other. I notice them adopting each other's mannerisms and repeating things that I definitely didn't teach them. Each of my kids is as different as the day is long. They each have their unique gifts, and the others benefit tremendously from them. My eldest teaches them to be sensitive. My middle guy teaches them to be brave. And my youngest teaches them to be patient.

Even when they don't get along (which is often), deep down I'm actually okay with it—this is *supposed* to happen. They are my little bear cubs learning to deal with conflict in a healthy way. They're learning to stand up for themselves and work out problems—great life skills they'll use later.

> They'll take care of each other.

They have fun together.

Watching my kids catch the giggles together fills my heart. It gets a little loud, yes, but it's so heartwarming to see them make each other laugh. They invent games, watch movies, build forts, blow bubbles, and sometimes just wander around the backyard. Built-in buddies for life.

I worry a lot about *creating* fun for them, about *making* magic that they'll remember when they're grown. The truth is, the real magic happens in the nooks and crannies of our days when we're simply together. When I see all three of them huddled over the same book. Or when I look in the rearview mirror and see them making silly faces at each other. Or when they hold hands and all shout "One-two-three!" before jumping into a pile of leaves. *That* is the stuff.

They'll take care of each other.

It gives my heart peace to know that my kids will have each other. With luck, they're forming bonds now that will last a lifetime. In that way, I know I'll always be with them.

Our little piece of the world is a far stretch from the Pinterest-esque existence I imagined. There is often at least one person crying, a seemingly endless cycle of losing shoes and losing patience, a fairly constant din of chaos. But the absolute bliss of witnessing the love between my children makes every second of the madness worth it.

The Rawness of Motherhood

COLLEEN TEMPLE

I brought my third daughter home from the hospital three weeks ago. *And just as my heart proved its wild and wonderful ability to expand when I had my second daughter, it did it yet again. I felt full of all the love in the world.*

I have always felt things very deeply. But as a mama, the feelings I have for my children are deeper and more raw than anything I've ever felt before.

I feel overwhelmed by parenting and protecting these little ones some days. Overwhelmed with love, with worry, with joy. There are scary, boring, and lonely times that I want to move past. Still, I'm in awe of it all.

As mothers, our hearts are fragile, open, and exposed—yet strong and fierce. Although these feelings come from the deepest love imaginable, sometimes I feel like I'm losing it.

I can go from wanting to pull my hair out with frustration and exhaustion at bedtime to wanting to wake my kids up because they're so cute and I miss them. I can go from forcing myself to calm down after asking my daughter to put her shoes on for the fifth time to melting into a pile of mush five seconds later when she tells her little sister that she's "*soooo* cute."

I can go from crying because it's been a hard day, no one's listening, and I don't know how I'm going to make it to the end of the day . . . to hugging and kissing on my kids because they worked together to color me a beautiful rainbow picture.

I know these feelings are nonsensical. Irrational. Up and down. All over the place. Yet they are my real and true feelings of motherhood.

To the mother who feels like she can't make sense of this wide range of feelings . . . who wants to bottle up the smell of her newborn . . . who wants to sit and stare at her baby's face for hours because she can't believe she made this gorgeous human—I'm that mama too.

To every mother who is exhausted at their 3:00 a.m. nursing wake-up call but so happy to hold her baby . . . who has heart palpitations when watching her partner hold, swaddle, and change a diaper . . . who feels she might explode with excitement while watching her child take their first steps—I'm that mama too.

To every mother who wants to jump and scream and clap with joy when they see their child kick a soccer ball at their first practice . . . who wants to give herself a hug when she checks on her sleeping children post-bedtime because today was a tough-as-nails day and she wonders if she was enough, did enough—I'm that mama too.

To every mother who doesn't want those toddler curls to *ever* disappear . . . who never wants to forget watching the I-just-learned-how-to-walk waddle . . . who wants to tuck that toddler giggle in her pocket forever . . . who leaves a parent-teacher conference beaming with pride because her child is "kind and helpful and confident"—I'm that mama too.

To every mother who wants to freeze time—I'm that mama too.

When you have a child, your heart cracks wide open. So, when you wonder if your heart can take any more, feel any more, or hold any more love, know that your wide-open heart can handle and hold more than you give it credit for.

It's all part of the magic of motherhood.

My Breastfeeding Miracle

JUDIE HARVEY

It was the first time my daughter was sick. At nine months, she got a terrible respiratory infection and was put on an asthma medicine that left her both wired and tired. For days she wouldn't eat, even though she loved all kinds of food and had been taking solids, drinking water, and having a bottle with formula during the day when I was at work. When I realized she hadn't wet her diaper in quite some time, I began to panic.

After taking her to the doctor, my husband and I took turns rocking her in her favorite chair, singing to her, distracting her with her favorite Dr. Seuss book, and trying to soothe her. But nothing was working.

How I wished I hadn't stopped breastfeeding.

Two weeks earlier, my daughter had shown signs that she wasn't as interested in nursing anymore. So I took the cue from her that it was time to taper off. Since she had only been nursing in the morning and evening, my breasts were flatter than pancakes at the height of her illness.

We'd gotten off to a very rocky start nursing. Nothing about breastfeeding was natural to me. Holding my baby close, skin to skin, was magic. Getting her to latch on properly? Agony. I figured that the miracle of breastfeeding I'd heard so much about must be a figment of postpartum euphoria.

The first three weeks included many days of tears and frustration for both of us. I was the first of my generation to breastfeed and remember my mother's deep-felt desire to give her first grandchild a bottle. I was tempted to forgo nursing but stuck with it for her. Eventually, my daughter found great comfort in nursing, and I even experienced that euphoric release.

I remember going to her two-week checkup and learning she'd gained weight. First, I created this beautiful, perfect child and now I had to keep her alive with *my body*? It was heady stuff. Seeing her limp, dehydrated body laboring to breathe, I felt desperate. Oh, how I wished I had milk for her.

After sending up a silent prayer, I put her to my breast.

I held her there, and she began to suck. She settled in and started to relax. My breasts were sore, but she was getting comfort, so I didn't care how much it hurt. As she finally drifted off and pulled away, I thought I saw milk on her lips. Hopeful thinking or blurry-eyed exhaustion? I wasn't sure until I woke up the next day.

Wondrously, overnight, my milk production kicked into gear. My breasts were slightly fuller, and I could feel that my milk ducts were producing milk. I nursed her around the clock for three days, feeding her exclusively with breast milk, literally watching her rehydrate and return to health. At the end of the three days, my body was providing everything she needed to literally stay alive—again.

I still get chills thinking about it.

Around the time I got pregnant, I had been told that I had a life-threatening health condition and might not be able to carry a child to term. This turned out to be untrue, but at the time I felt my body had betrayed me. I questioned its innate ability to bear and nurture children.

This experience showed me that my body was designed perfectly. Watching my daughter return to health, I regretted every time I had doubted my body (or criticized my cellulite and stretch marks). Because over those three days, my body showed me just how perfect and magical—and trustworthy—it truly is.

This Life Is a Privilege

COLLEEN TEMPLE

"Remember when you wanted what you currently have?" I saw that quote on social media the other night as I sat scrolling and rocking while I nursed my baby.

I remember the pre-mom me who loved the freedom of making plans on a whim or booking a trip without worrying whether the hotel had a crib or if I was packing enough diapers. I remember enjoying my life (of course) but was always looking toward the *next* part. The part when we'd get married. The part when we'd have kids.

And now, here I am knee-deep in the trenches of motherhood. I have the life I asked for. I have a four-year-old, a two-year-old, and a five-month-old. I work from home, writing about the joys of motherhood along with the heartaches and pain that get tangled up in the beauty of it all.

I am working diligently every day to raise good humans. Kind, compassionate, loving humans. Humans who will one day go out into this world and do something great. It's a huge undertaking, a ginormous responsibility.

But more than anything, motherhood is a privilege.

Mothering my three daughters is my greatest joy and will be the biggest, shiniest accomplishment of my life. It is my passion and my purpose. My heart and soul. It can't compete with any other milestone or award I may reach or receive, even if I were to win an Academy Award or complete the Boston Marathon.

They're why I dream, why I push myself, and why I constantly want to be better.

I remember when I wanted what I currently have. And the realization stopped me in my tracks when online the quote called out to me. The life I wanted was here. Right now. The role of mother *is* mine.

This moment of clarity brought forth a heart full of gratitude. I am grateful for the hardships and the successes. I am grateful for the problems and the solutions.

This aha moment was interrupted by my daughter calling, "Mama! Come look at what I made!" My very proud four-year-old was holding up a portrait. "Look at how beautiful you are, Mommy!" At the same time, my middle daughter was "cleaning" up all of our shoes (in other words, taking them out of the designated shoe bucket and spreading them all over the floor). "Look, Mommy! I'm a helper!"

The messy room raised my anxiety antenna a bit, but the girls' enthusiasm and earnestness won me over—as it always does.

I *get* to be their mom.

These awesome kids are *my* kids. I get to teach them things. I get to hug them and make them laugh. I get to know what's in their hearts. I get to help shape who they will become.

When it's all said and done and my time on earth ends, I will know my truth. My truth is the all-consuming love I have for my kids. My truth is the beauty of watching them blossom and the pain of being needed less with every ounce of independence they gain.

My truth is that motherhood has transformed me—mind, body, and soul—into the person I was always destined to be.

So yes, I remember when I wanted what I currently have. But I never knew it was going to be *this* amazing. This rewarding. This fulfilling. Motherhood is hard. But it is truly the greatest privilege of my life.

To the Person Who Falls In Love with My Son

DIANA SPALDING

To the person who falls in love with my son,

I'm not sure when exactly I'll be giving you this letter. Maybe in a few decades, on the day you marry my son, or maybe on a random day that feels right. Whenever it is, I hope I'll be alive and well enough to fully experience how happy I am to know you.

Right now, it feels a little silly to be writing this letter. My toddler is upstairs, tucked in bed, lost in a sea of blankets lovingly wrapped around him. But he's going to grow up faster than I am prepared for. Before I know it, he'll sleep in a new bed, in a different home, away from me.

Somewhere along the way, he will find you. And everything will change.

Right now, he chooses *me* to play race cars and read books with. He likes *my* lunches better than the school's. He wants *me* to be the last one to kiss him goodnight. But one day, he'll choose *you*. He'll want to spend his days off with *you*, go on adventures with *you*, cook for *you*.

Right now, his eyes light up with joy when he sees me, and it never ever gets old. But one day those eyes will sparkle for you. He'll study your hands, memorize your face, and have pictures of you up in his office.

Right now, I am his hero. He asks me for help. He snuggles with me when he's sick. But one day, you will be his hero. He'll ask a question, you and I will each give him a different answer, and he'll listen to yours over mine. You'll help him discover the world and be the one to make him feel better when he's sad or sick.

Right now, I'm teaching him how to be kind, how to respect others and be respected. How to listen, how to help, and how to ask for help when he needs it. One day, I hope he will lavish you with that same respect and kindness.

Right now, home is with me. But one day, he'll be at home wherever he is with you.

And that's okay. It's my honor to be his mother, to help guide him as he grows into the person you will fall in love with. It will be my honor to know you as well. I want you to know that if you treat him well and make him happy, I will love you no matter your gender, race, ethnicity, or religion.

I promise to try to find a balance between being in your lives and being helpful. No pop-ins, I swear. I promise (to try) not to give advice unless you ask.

And to you, the person who has fallen in love with my son, I promise to fall in love with you too. Because the person who loves my son will understand what's behind those sparkling eyes of his, like I do. That person will think his raspy voice is adorable and laugh at his jokes.

So, how could I not love the person who loves all of that about my child?

Right now, while I have him, before he is yours, I'll cherish every moment, every kiss, and every snuggle. And one day, when you love him and he loves you, I'll be so proud. Proud of the person he has become, proud of the person he has chosen to spend his days with, and so proud to be his mom.

Love,
Mama

The World Changed When I Became a Mother

KARELL ROXAS

Time stood still briefly and infinitely the moment you were born. Looking back, life seemed so different before and after becoming a mother. It changed me forever.

They said it would. There were warnings. Happy stories and sad ones, heartfelt advice, and people looking deep into my pregnant eyes, trying to convey just how massive this shift would be.

I naïvely thought I understood.

I listened, nodded my head, and tried to imagine how different life could be. But in my imagination, the only difference was you—not me.

I pictured you in places I knew a baby would be: The crib we were assembling in your nursery? A sleeping baby is lying there. The play mat bought from the store? You again, doing tummy time. Even the future beyond the newborn phase was obvious. There you were, a little older, sitting in the high chair. I could see you so clearly. I could even imagine you fussing. I believed I knew it all.

But I overlooked something so obvious to me now that I almost laugh: How I would *feel*.

I felt fragile the day you were born.

Not because my body and mind had just been pushed to the edge of their limitations, but because I felt like I was suddenly inside out. Out of nowhere, pieces of what had only ever been private—my DNA, my heart, my blood—existed publicly, outside of my body.

I felt strong the day you were born.

Powerful, even. *I just did that!* I brought a new life into this world, safely and bravely.

This finale of forty weeks and two days of gestation resulted in absolute wonder at what we as women are capable of. I can overcome. I am made of the right stuff. I am masterful.

I felt connected the day you were born.

In bearing you, I felt my sudden humanity and mortality. I felt a shared experience with my mother, my grandmother, my great-grandmother, and all the others who came before her. I felt like I discovered a thread that had been there all along, connecting this new life to lives past and to future generations. I suddenly felt part of a new club. I understood what "mother" really meant. I *got* it.

I felt
connected
the day you
were born.

I felt raw the day you were born.

It was as if suddenly all the emotions in the past decades of being alive had been muted. The previous ups and downs of heartbreak and joy were mere shadows of what I could feel. *This* is ecstasy. *This* is fear. *This* is pride. *This* is infatuation.

My fingertips tingled as if touching everything for the very first time. Feeling each sharp edge or soft place. I was suddenly sensitive to every sound, every breath, every hiccup around me. My vision sharpened. Colors deepened. I was awakened and more alive than ever before.

The world and how I travel through it now is profoundly different than it was before you were born. But I understand it now. A new life can't be introduced to the world without having a profound impact. As a thrown rock creates a ripple in the stillness of a lake, this new soul shifts and transforms everything it touches . . . until suddenly there's no returning to who you were before.

practice
FINDING THE MAGIC MOMENTS OF MOTHERHOOD

RACHEL GORTON

The secret is out: Motherhood can be hard. *Really* hard. But the secret we don't talk about enough is that it's also full of pure magic. I write this as I watch my son quietly sit in the corner and read his third book this month. Just a few months ago, I couldn't pay him to read. I know these are the moments I must hold on to. The moments where I can cherish the sweet silence and the wonder in his eyes as he learns something new. Because when I stop to appreciate these moments, I realize they bring me *so much joy*. They show me the true magic of motherhood.

These big moments are beyond our wildest dreams and there is magic right around us at all times. Maybe your big moments are in the way you observe your child concentrating on building a block tower—full of focus and determination. Maybe it's in the way he gently rubs your back when you pick him up. Maybe it's found when your daughter holds your hand as you watch *Finding Dory*. Or when you watch your child take in a new experience.

Sometimes it's hard to see even the most beautiful things right in front of us, especially when we're clouded with chaos or blinded by the monotony of life. But we can find the magic too, with a simple meditation.

Give yourself fifteen minutes to pause and revel in this experience of noticing the wonder that is your life.

1. Find somewhere to sit or lie down where you can feel relaxed. Take a second to get settled and then begin by taking three or four deep breaths.

2. Close your eyes if that feels natural to you. Allow yourself to appreciate the silence. Appreciate how good it feels to be by yourself. Appreciate the space you need away from the day-to-day to be able to honor the beauty of your life.

3. Now, sort through some memories. Bring yourself back to the very minute you came face-to-face with your child. Allow yourself to feel that wonder again. Remember saying to yourself, *Is this real?*

4. Recall when you heard your child say "Mama" for the first time. Where were you? What season was it? Let yourself revel in how special that made you feel. These moments will forever be yours.

5. As you take this time and settle into your meditation, reflect on the wonder and magic of your life and simply breathe. With each inhale, breathe in the beauty of all these sweet memories and hold the inhale for an extra moment while you savor them. With each exhale, smile softly and allow these precious moments to soothe you. Repeat, slowly inhaling and exhaling.

Come back to this meditation any time you feel like you've lost the magic of motherhood. Bring back the joy-filled, real memories of your journey and open your eyes up to the small, everyday moments of wonder around you. The magic is always here.

journal QUESTIONS

For the next week, take time each day to reflect on the magic of motherhood with the following prompts. Notice these moments and write them down. The practice of seeing and noticing is one of the greatest gifts of the motherhood journey.

- In which moments of motherhood do you feel most alive?

- Contemplate your day today—what were your small moments of magic?

- When do you have the most fun with your children? What do you love to do with them?

- What does being a mother mean to you?

Conclusion

The Superpower of Mothers—Getting It Done

COLLEEN TEMPLE

As the editor of this book, I've laughed, cried, and relived my own parenting moments while reading these beautiful essays from moms around the world. I'm so grateful for this community of mothers who have been willing to share their stories—their successes and challenges, their highs and lows.

Many stories here are the result of mama superpowers.

Eloquently expressing the truths of motherhood: superpower. Sharing all that we accomplish in one day: superpower. Managing to function on a daily basis while carrying around the weight of this all-encompassing love, this overwhelming feeling of being needed at *all* times, this urgency to keep our kids safe every minute of every day: superpower.

I have a four-year-old, a two-year-old, and a five-month-old. They are busy and fun and energetic! And, during the creation of this book, we were between childcare, experiencing a winter of repeated blizzards and power outages, and combating numerous stomach bugs. I often found myself working thirty-plus-hour weeks from home with children crawling on me. I've accepted help from my in-laws, sisters, and parents, taken calls in the car while my kids napped, and finally found a babysitter we all love.

While I'm not juggling all these balls perfectly, they *are* all staying in the air at the same time (so far). I never imagined motherhood would turn me into a juggler, but thinking about the circus seems all too real: I often feel like the ringmaster and the tightrope walker. (Which makes sense because motherhood most certainly *is* the greatest show on earth.)

But I am getting it done. And I'm proud to be showing up every day. My friend and cofounder of Motherly, Liz, recently lovingly compared me to a duck. She said, "You're paddling away underwater—fast, fast, fast—but you look so cool and calm on the surface, like you're just gliding away."

Liz, thank you. I'm not always cool or calm. I am the exact opposite most days. But I *have* realized something during my four-plus years of motherhood: I can get it done. It's one of my mama superpowers. No matter how busy or chaotic life is, if something needs to be done, I muster up the strength and I get it done. Whether that means I have to ask for help or stay up late—it's on.

I imagine a lot of you are nodding along as you read this. Because we are mothers—we get things done. Each of us is bringing our individual strengths to our role of mom every day, to be the very best version of ourselves for our children.

Let's name what we're good at and own it.

We may not share the same powers as the popular superheroes we know and love, but our specific talents and specialties are impressive, nonetheless. Our superpowers change lives. They *make* lives!

I have the ability to shower, feed everyone breakfast, get everyone dressed, find everyone's shoes, and buckle three children in car seats before I've even had my second cup of coffee.

I have the ability to pack for a weekend away, plan a birthday party, and clean my house in one afternoon.

I have the ability to make dinner, empty the dishwasher, and finish an email while simultaneously leading a dance party.

I have the ability to breastfeed my baby while meeting a work deadline at the same time I'm finding the "good" episode of *Daniel Tiger* for my toddler.

I have the ability to change a blowout diaper in the car with only three wipes left—in record time—while also singing "Let It Go" (on key, mind you).

I have the ability to calm my wired preschooler down at bedtime just by lying in her bed with her—and with a cuddle and a song, my energetic kiddo is sound asleep.

I have the ability to wipe tears, solve sibling squabbles, and turn frowns upside down in a matter of minutes.

I have the ability to see the future of this world through the eyes of my children—and know I have the ability to influence it.

Motherhood takes superhuman strength because it requires everything we've got: mind, body, soul.

Giving birth requires strength. Signing adoption papers requires strength. Finding a surrogate requires strength. Healing from a miscarriage requires strength. Figuring out how to be a mother requires strength. Navigating a partnership *and* parenting requires strength. Extending ourselves grace in those less-than-proud moments requires strength. Waking up after another exhausting night to face another demanding day requires strength.

And you have that strength inside of you.

How do I know? Because this is motherhood. It's a willingness to step up to the mind-bending challenge of raising helpless tiny babies into confident, capable adults. And the only way we can get there is by finding our superpowers, being honest about our limitations, and then knowing when we need to ask for help. I mean, even superheroes have sidekicks, right?

Strength and superpowers, mama.

You have them inside of you . . . and you always will.

Thanks for being on this wonderful, wild, and incredibly powerful ride with me. Because *this* is motherhood.

XO,
Colleen

Authors

Jill Koziol is the cofounder and CEO of Motherly. She resides in Silicon Valley with her husband and two daughters.

Liz Tenety is the cofounder and chief digital officer of Motherly. She resides with her husband and three children in the New York City suburbs.

Colleen Temple is the MotherlyStories editor at Motherly and resides in the Boston suburbs with her husband and three daughters.

Contributors

Jenn Press Arata is the author of the children's book *Sweet Dreams*, a TV personality, and the creator of the food and lifestyle blog *That's So Jenn!* (thatssojenn.com). She lives in Connecticut with her husband and their much-wished-for daughter, Emma, and son, Josh.

Raschael Ash is a freelance writer at reimaginingrascal.com and resides in Alberta, Canada, with her partner, three children, two dogs, and one cat.

Denaye Barahona, PhD, is the voice behind *Simple Families*—a blog, podcast, and community that helps mothers thrive through simple living. She lives in New York with her husband and two children.

Beth Berry is a writer, life coach for awakening women, and mother of four daughters. You can find her exploring the mountains around Asheville, North Carolina, or at revolutionfromhome.com.

Allie Casazza married her junior high algebra partner and is a mom to their four young kids. She is the founder and host of *The Purpose Show* podcast and creator of Your Uncluttered Home, an online decluttering course that has earned her national attention for her philosophy of simple motherhood and simple living.

Maria Confer is the founder of Wildflower Liberty League and lives in Boulder, Colorado, with her husband and son.

Kayla Craig writes in the margins of motherhood as she and her husband raise four young kids who joined their family via birth and adoption. They live in Iowa, where Kayla makes room for new friends at the table and old books on the shelf. Connect at kaylacraig.com.

Tanika White Davis is a writer, reader, and chocolate lover who makes her living "in communications." She and her husband live in Baltimore with their eight-year-old twin sons and six-year-old daughter.

Erica DeSpain is the author of *Whimsical September*, a popular family and lifestyle blog for women. She adores her husband and two daughters and resides in Huntsville, Alabama.

Catherine Dietrich is a former magazine journalist and a mama of two. A British South African, she currently lives in Switzerland with her husband and two small daughters. She writes for various online publications as well as her blog, *Littles, Love and Sunshine*, about the wonderfully ordinary moments of motherhood.

Rebecca Eanes is the bestselling author of several books on positive parenting, as well as the parenting editor at Motherly. She is nestled in the beautiful Appalachian Mountains with her husband and two sons.

Anne-Marie Gambelin is Motherly's features editor. She resides in the Silicon Valley with her husband, Don, their daughter, and two sons.

Emily Glover is the senior news writer at Motherly. She lives in Colorado with her husband and two children.

Sara Goldstein is a brand editor at Motherly and is officially shorter than one of her two kids. She spends an inordinate amount of time thinking about how to tell oft-repeated stories in new ways.

Rachel Gorton is the business development director and resident sleep expert at Motherly. She lives outside of Boston with her husband and three children.

Erica L. Green is a national correspondent for the *New York Times*, covering education. She lives in Baltimore County with her husband Matthew, two children Everly and Ezra, and dog-daughter Sadie.

Judie Harvey is an editor and writer of health and lifestyle books, blogs, and book-marketing and publicity material. She is the mom of three grown children, has a black belt in tae kwon do, and lives in southeast Florida.

Jamie Henderson is a single mother of a son who is on the autism spectrum. She runs a Facebook page called "Autism Life with Jaxon," where she shares their story in hopes that more people will become aware and accepting of autism.

Sydney Hutt is an English major and future high school teacher. She lives in a suburb outside of Vancouver, Canada, with her partner, cat, and identical twin daughters.

Jessica Johnston is a mama to four kids and writes about the raw truths of motherhood at wonderoak.com.

Alicia Keswani is a working mom who is raising two daughters (and a mischievous, sock-stealing dog) with her husband in Chicago, Illinois.

Amber Leventry is a writer and LGBTQ advocate. She lives in Vermont with her partner and their three kids.

Erin Leyba, LCSW, PhD, is the author of the new book *Joy Fixes for Weary Parents: 101 Quick, Research-Based Ways to Overcome Stress and Build a Life You Love*. She is a therapist in private practice (www.erinleyba.com) and lives in the Chicago, Illinois area with her husband and four kids.

Justine Lorelle LoMonaco is the brand editor at Motherly. She lives in a tiny town in Virginia with her husband and two children.

Kelly May is the owner of Salon Orlee, where she's also a stylist. She resides with her husband and daughter on Long Island, New York.

Brianna Mobilian is the owner of The Prana Tribe (thepranatribe.com) and resides in sunny Florida with her husband and two children.

Megan O'Neill is a lactation counselor and stay-at-home mom. She and her husband reside in the Boston suburbs with their two sons and daughter. She is an autism advocate, makeup lover, and yogi.

Courtney Rochowicz is a wife, mom to one beloved little boy, and Motherly's studios editor. A Midwesterner at heart, she lives in Manhattan with her family. Of all the things she loves to do, motherhood might be her favorite role of all.

Azizah Rowen is a California-bred New Yorker, musician, actress, and freelance writer. She is also an ambassador for the March of Dimes and resides in Marin County, California, with her husband and two sons.

Karell Roxas is the editor-in-chief at Motherly and lives in New Jersey with her two favorite men—her husband and her son.

Rasha Rushdy is a coffee-loving, world-traveling, library-frequenting mother of two who appreciates a good pun and unexpected meaningful conversations. She started *The Tuna Chronicles* in 2015 on a whim, which reignited her love of writing.

Diana Spalding is a midwife and Motherly's digital education editor. She lives outside Philadelphia with her husband, three children, and dog.

Jacqueline Munro Tapp is the lead video producer at Motherly. She is a producer, director, writer, and birth doula. She lives in New Jersey with her family.

Cait Thrasher is raising two awesome autistic kids in northern Virginia with her husband, Matt, and works from home as an architectural draftsman.

Carolyn Wagner is a psychotherapist in private practice who specializes in trauma and maternal mental health. She lives in Chicago, Illinois, with her husband and three children.

Ashley Wasilenko is the distribution partnerships manager at Motherly. She was born and raised in New Jersey, where she currently lives with her wonderful husband and two adorable sons. She is an avid cook and lover of peonies.

Juli Williams is Motherly's brand photographer. She is a photographer and content creator who lives with her husband and two children in Miami, Florida.

Jessica Wimer is a labor and delivery nurse, an international board-certified lactation consultant (IBCLC), and a mother of two. In her nonexistent spare time, she writes breastfeeding and postpartum support articles for her blog, *Born and Fed*. Jessica resides in the beautiful country acres of Lancaster, Pennsylvania, with her husband and two children.

About Motherly

Motherly is a modern lifestyle brand redefining motherhood. We exist to change the world on behalf of a new generation of mothers, engaging a 15M+ audience each month as the only expert-driven, woman-centered, non-judgmental, and empowering parenting brand. Blurring digital and physical boundaries, Motherly's product line launches in 2019. Motherly was founded in 2015 by Jill Koziol, consultant/repeat entrepreneur, and Liz Tenety, an award-winning *Washington Post* editor and digital strategist.

To learn more, please visit Mother.ly or follow us on Facebook at /motherlymedia and Instagram at /mother.ly.

M MOTHERLY

About Sounds True

Sounds True is a multimedia publisher whose mission is to inspire and support personal transformation and spiritual awakening. Founded in 1985 and located in Boulder, Colorado, we work with many of the leading spiritual teachers, thinkers, healers, and visionary artists of our time. We strive with every title to preserve the essential "living wisdom" of the author or artist. It is our goal to create products that not only provide information to a reader or listener, but that also embody the quality of a wisdom transmission.

For those seeking genuine transformation, Sounds True is your trusted partner. At SoundsTrue.com you will find a wealth of free resources to support your journey, including exclusive weekly audio interviews, free downloads, interactive learning tools, and other special savings on all our titles.

To learn more, please visit SoundsTrue.com/freegifts or call us toll-free at 800.333.9185.

 sounds true